# THEATRE SYMPOSIUM
## A JOURNAL OF THE SOUTHEASTERN THEATRE CONFERENCE

# Theatrical Spaces and Dramatic Places

## *The Reemergence of the Theatre Building in the Renaissance*

### *Volume 4*

*Published by the*

Southeastern Theatre Conference and

The University of Alabama Press

THEATRE SYMPOSIUM is published annually by the South-eastern Theatre Conference, Inc. (SETC), and by The University of Alabama Press. SETC nonstudent members receive the journal as a part of their membership under rules determined by SETC. For information on membership, write to SETC, P.O. Box 9868, Greensboro, NC 27429–0868. *All other inquiries* regarding sub-scriptions, circulation, purchase of individual copies, and requests to reprint materials should be addressed to The University of Alabama Press, Box 870380, Tuscaloosa, AL 35487–0380.

THEATRE SYMPOSIUM publishes works of scholarship resulting from a single-topic meeting held on a southeastern university cam-pus each spring. A call for papers to be presented at that meeting is widely publicized each autumn for the following spring. Authors are therefore not encouraged to send unsolicited manuscripts directly to the editor. Information about the next symposium is available from the editor, Paul C. Castagno, Department of Theatre, University of Alabama, Box 870239, Tuscaloosa, AL 35487–0239.

# THEATRE SYMPOSIUM
## A JOURNAL OF THE SOUTHEASTERN THEATRE CONFERENCE

Volume 4                    *Contents*                    *1996*

# Introduction

IN ITS AIM, excellence of participants, and range of articles dealing with the early modern period, it is my hope that Volume 4 of *Theatre Symposium* makes a substantial contribution to theatre studies. As in previous volumes, Part I is made up of essays from the invited symposium panelists followed by a discussion, which is transcribed and edited. Part II consists of articles from symposium participants around the topic of specialized interest, which are refereed by the Editorial Board. The goal of Part I is to examine the reemergence of theatre building across the broad European spectrum during the sixteenth and seventeenth centuries. Each scholar selected and herein published represents the epitome of their discipline: Andrew Gurr, Elizabethan stage and the new Globe; John Allen, Spanish Golden Age theatres; Virginia Scott, French theatre in the age of Louis XIV; Luigi Allegri, Teatro Farnese—Italian Renaissance theatre; Ronald Vince, historiography and bibliography.

This extraordinary panel was put together by Theatre Symposium Conference Coordinators Stanley Longman and Franklin Hildy of the University of Georgia. An expert in the Italian Renaissance theatre, Professor Longman provides the inaugural essay that serves as a springboard to Part I. Professor Hildy, the American scholar who is most associated with the new Globe project, is widely published in this area and contributes to Part II. The internationally represented conference was held on 7 and 8 April 1995 and hosted by the Department of Drama at the University of Georgia. Participants and observers found the scholarship, discussions, and diversions simply first-rate. It is in this refined, published format that we present the scholarship to you.

The juried papers selected for Part II reflect a broader range of topics, dealing with aspects of theatrical space or dramatic place and progressing from the late medieval, through Renaissance, Mannerist, and baroque periods. The Italian theatre is represented in four essays. Thomas Pallen's article discusses the Renaissance notion of dressing not only the stage but the entire theatre and entry areas; Thomas Connolly reexamines the putative notions of academic theatre at Vicenza; Frank Mohler deciphers the very complicated, albeit striking baroque practice of moving flying scenery from upstage to downstage; and I discuss spatial practices in early *commedia dell'arte* iconography as stemming from a Mannerist aesthetic. On the English theatre, Franklin Hildy offers some stunning insights into Elizabethan oppositional staging, while August Staub and Rhona Justice-Malloy reevaluate the late medieval stage and concept of theatre within the context of Scholasticism. Offering new insight into the Spanish Golden Age, John Dowling introduces us to the previously underresearched Buen Retiro theatre in Madrid, Spain. The illustrations throughout this edition clarify the picture of this rich visual period in theatre history.

A most significant debate in current theatre history is dealt with in this volume: that is, the problem of re-creating the historical past through the forms of reconstructed theatre structures, such as the recently completed Globe stage. How are such reconstructions valuable? In what ways do they validate or contradict appropriate theatre research? What about the problematic aspect of audiences? Throwing down the gauntlet, Ronald Vince posited that through the actual process of reconstruction, the quotation marks around the "new Globe" will fall away, disappearing entirely within a few months or years. What will exist by the time of this publication as the new Globe will just stand in for the historical Globe, becoming definitive as the "way it actually was" in Shakespeare's time. John Allen pointed out the caveat when he brought our attention to the erroneous Comba model of the Spanish *corrales* theatre, which nevertheless has stood and continues to stand as its putative model. The presence of scholars, such as Gurr and Hildy, who are part of the team behind the new Globe, made exchanges more interesting and, at times, heated (see "Symposium Discussion").

Volume 4 represents the final year in my two-year term as editor of *Theatre Symposium*. As one of its founders, I served as associate editor for two years and have been the Symposium director of two conferences: our first, on *commedia dell'arte;* and the third, which I coordinated with the Literary Managers and Dramaturgs of the Americas (LMDA)—"Voice of the Dramaturg." During the past four to five years the journal has achieved a national reputation, attracted some of the top scholars nationally and internationally, and carved a niche for itself in the area of theatre studies. The Editorial Board represents excellence in all areas of theatre studies and has been most helpful in its responses. What has been most rewarding for me is the blend of scholarly intensity and intimacy at each conference made possible by the focused subject matter. This concentration makes the journal particularly useful in the classroom, particularly in the upper-level seminar class. Editing and sharpening the writing, and producing this work with the considerable help of The University of Alabama Press, has been most gratifying. I now turn editorship over to my highly respected colleague, Stanley Longman, who steps over from his position on the Editorial Board.

I wish to thank previous editor Philip Hill for his continued work, as well as Associate Editors David Frankel and Steven Hart for lightening a sometimes very heavy load. Assistant Editor Bert Wallace did a yeoman's job in implementing the edits and preparing the manuscript for presentation to The University of Alabama Press. Our outstanding Editorial Board provided excellent suggestions on many articles. The University of Alabama Press should be commended for its fine work on all the past volumes, and for dealing with some of the concerns inherent in this volume—the considerable reliance on illustrations, for example. Thanks to the Southeastern Theatre Conference (SETC) and the Publications Committee (PUBCOM). I hope that I have served you well, and I appreciate your faith in me.

Finally, I want to express my deepest and sincerest thanks and love to Molly, my wife, for her considerable patience during the many hours I was away from the family working on the journal.

PAUL C. CASTAGNO
*Editor*

All translations are by the authors unless otherwise indicated.

# The Idea of the Playhouse

## Stanley V. Longman

S OME TWENTY YEARS AGO, a distinguished professor of comparative literature at the University of Georgia published an essay in the local newspaper arguing the case against staging plays. He asserted that plays, like all varieties of fiction, depend on the creation of an imagined world that the reader can conjure much more richly in the mind than all the canvas, boards, greasepaint, and flesh can do upon the stage. My Hamlet and my Elsinore are better than yours (at least for me), and both of ours are better than any producer can put up on the rickety platform they call the stage. It is a kind of solipsistic romantic vision. But there was also something deeply disturbing about the essay, partly because it was eloquently written, but mostly because it missed a powerful dimension of the drama—and the writer must have been the poorer for it. Yes, we have all witnessed productions of plays that fell short of capturing their worlds fully and richly. The leading actress just did not look the part; somebody's fake beard distracted us; a wheel on one of the scenic wagons squeaked; or the canvas shook when the door slammed. Yet, we have all encountered moments in the theatre that have transported us outside ourselves, moments that were rich because they were so immediate, and because they were shared with a crowd. "Being there" constitutes a powerful ingredient in theatrical experiences. Reading *Hamlet* is clearly not a case of "being there."

Theatre depends on people being there. Anyone who has been through the rehearsal process knows the sensation of a play hungering for an audience. And the encounter between play and audience is often one that enlarges and enhances the play in directions no one could fully predict. The dramatic counterpart to that old philosophical conundrum, "If a tree falls in the forest and no one is there, does it make a sound?"

is, "If a play is presented and no one is there, is it a play?" In the most meaningful and human sense, the answer in both instances is no. Plays, like sound, take on meaning only in the encounter. Thornton Wilder offers an appropriate description of this in his essay "Some Thoughts on Playwriting":

> The theatre partakes of the nature of festival. Life imitated is life elevated to a higher power. In the case of comedy the vitality of these pretended surprises, deceptions, and *contretemps* becomes so lively that before a spectator, solitary, or regarding himself as solitary, the structure of so much event would inevitably expose the artificiality of the attempt and ring hollow and unjustified; and in the case of tragedy, the accumulation of woe and apprehension would soon fall short of conviction. (111)

The very assemblage of an audience produces a resonance elevating the dramatic experience to a new plane. Theatre is as much an art form as it is a social institution. Indeed, its artistic effect depends on its social context. People come together to perform a play for people who have come together to witness it. Artistic effect emerges out of that coming together. This condition has inspired interesting developments in the direction of a sociology of the theatre in the hands of Jean Duvignaud and others, just as anthropology took interest in the ritual roots of theatre, as in the work of Victor Turner.

This social dimension of dramatic art virtually demands some form of playing space set over against some form of attending space that organizes the relationship between spectacle and spectator. Somehow, the interaction of performer and audience must be provided for. It may consist simply of an open space at the foot of a hillside, as it once did. The spectacle may be in front of us or in our midst; it may even shift its ground, now here and now there. But however it exists, it respects some established pattern. That pattern involves manipulation of three distinct areas: spectacle space, spectator space, and neutral space. For convenience, we might call them stage, house, and tiring-house. The playhouse is an architectural statement of these relationships. Ironically, the first of the three areas to be given architectural expression would seem to have been the tiring-house: the Greek *skene*. Once the Greeks had provided for the neutral area into which actors could retire and attire themselves, the idea of a playhouse began to develop.

This matter of the tiring-house actually introduces a second impor-tant dimension to the theatre. The theatre depends, in a sense, on a double edge. It derives meaning not only through its social dimension —organizing the relationship between spectacle and spectator—but also through the manipulation of an actual space occupied by actual people into an imagined domain populated by characters. The spectacle-spectator dichotomy is complemented by another dichotomy, that of the actual and the virtual. Where we have the stage, we also have the world of the play. Where we see an actor perform on that stage, we sense a character living in a distinct world. Where we hear talk of horses, we think we see them. We are, as Shakespeare requested in the prologue of *Henry V*, to work on "our imaginary forces." The tiring-house contributes handily to the actual-virtual dichotomy. At the same time, it is a physical convenience, a neutral ground into which the actors may retreat or out of which they may emerge, and an unseen extension of the virtual world of the play. When the actor disappears into the tiring-house, the character has gone somewhere else in the play's world. Oedipus goes into his palace where he puts out his eyes; Old Hamlet returns to his limbo; Tartuffe is hauled off to prison; Hedwig takes a gun into the wild duck's attic and kills herself; and Tilden goes out to the backyard and digs up the buried child. In each of these instances, a very different sort of playhouse is implied. Dramatic places must find expression in the theatrical spaces.

The idea of the playhouse, then, entails some systematic expression of places through architectural articulation of space. It calls for the creation of a spatial relationship between the players and the audience as well as for a dynamic arrangement to play on the collective imagination. A visit to a well-designed playhouse, even when it is empty, can be a vivid and powerful experience, for it will inevitably embody a vivid sense of the exchange of energy between performers and audience as well as rich implications of the worlds it was intended to contain.

On this score, despite their physical similarities, the Greek theatre was much different from the Roman. While both structures, especially the Roman, served as models for the theatre of the Renaissance, these later theatres ultimately bore little kinship with them. The Greek theatre was a four-part construction: the *skene,* or tiring-house; the *logeion,* or stage; the *theatron,* or seeing place; and the *orchestra,* or dancing area. The fourth space, the orchestra, accommodated the chorus. The chorus functioned both as performer in the play—engaging the actors, singing, and dancing—and as audience, responding to the play often in ways at odds with the *theatron* audience. That audience surrounding the orchestra area gained a strong sense of their shared vision. Moreover, the view out across the countryside beyond the *skene* served as a reminder of the larger world beyond the play, the world ruled by the gods. The Roman theatre, by contrast, was a self-contained, tripartite structure (tiring-house, stage, and audience area) much more given to frontal presentation and closed off from the outside world. The stage looked and functioned very much like a city street.

The last Roman theatre was probably built sometime in the fourth century. With Christian animosity to the theatre and the Emperor Constantine's conversion, such public structures rapidly became moribund. Naturally, theatrical activity continued, but, no longer formalized as a social institution, it went on without a playhouse. We were not to encounter a new permanent playhouse for more than a millennium, not until the second half of the sixteenth century.

When the new playhouses began to be constructed, they assumed a variety of shapes. There were no immediate models from which to base the new structures. Yet, theatrical activity resumed with great vigor from the fifteenth century onward, eventually providing some paradigms for the new theatrical structures. Indeed, that had been the case with the constructing of classical theatres as well. The Greek playhouses did not go up until the fourth century B.C., well after the greatest Greek plays had been produced, while the Roman theatres were built more than a hundred years after Plautus and Terence. Renaissance playhouses tended to formalize contemporary theatrical conventions based on medieval stage practices. This formalization is especially true of the Elizabethan open-air public playhouses and Spanish *corrales*. The French, who built the first playhouse of the new age, the *Hôtel de Bourgogne* in 1548, followed a similar pattern but retreated indoors to converted spaces, often former tennis courts. These three countries developed playhouses out of a professional and commercial need: the theatre had become a profession, and eventually such institutions needed a fixed structure—a playhouse. The Italian playhouses, on the other hand, developed independently of the professional theatre, apart from the *commedia dell'arte,* and responded to the special requirements of learned academies and the courts. Thus, the Italians were more fully revolutionary, at least ostensibly breaking from medieval practices. They combined the classical models and their new philosophical outlook to create a very new theatre structure.

Ultimately, the Renaissance presented two very distinct types of playhouse—one associated with the English, the other with the Italian. At almost every point they are in sharp contrast with each other. The English theatre is based on a kind of Chinese box principle, whereas the Italian structure concerns the idea of a window open to another world.

The Chinese box appears in the Elizabethan playhouse as worlds contained within worlds contained within worlds. The outside world and the extended world of the play surround the house itself, while the galleries and pit surround most of the stage area. Within the stage area, the private lives of the characters exist inside the overt behavior of the actors. Another phrase from *Henry V*'s prologue applies here: "Suppose within the girdle of these walls are now confined two mighty monarchies." The theatre structure is virtually a paradigm of the cosmos—the heavens, as they were actually called, encased in the attic above the stage; hell interred below the stage trapdoors; and, naturally, Earth represented in the space between. The stage area itself functioned in an emblematic manner: objects, doorways, windows, balconies all served as signs or emblems of other, imagined things. In this respect, the Elizabethans clearly continued and formalized medieval stage practices. The Elizabethan stage was essentially a *platea,* a generalized acting area, representing one place, then another. The multiple points of entry onto the stage (balcony, window, alcove, door, trap, etc.) were generalized mansions. A character appearing on the balcony would call attention to what this new place was to be. The audience would be satisfied when an actor described the arrival of ships from Venice as he spied them from the ramparts of the Cyprus fort. This construct of dramatic place is not much different from seeing performers appear out of a mansion labeled "Pontius Pilate's Palace," then walk onto the open *platea.* When the English playhouse generalized and encased the mansions within the playhouse walls, the theatre truly became the world in miniature. This notion gives added meaning to Shakespeare's "all the world's a stage."

On the other hand, the Italian playhouse emerged partly as a deliberate effort to recreate the ancient theatre, partly as an expression of its social function, but mostly as a response to new perceptions of the world and its space. It is in that latter connection that the principle of theatre as window aptly applies. Because of its newfound fascination with three-dimensional space, the Italian theatre is not so much emblematic as it is illusionistic. The false perspective manipulation of space was based on a perception of mankind in the context of earthly life. This intense fascination with spatial manipulation led naturally to the characterizing of stage space as a vision beyond a window. The audience viewed its city streets while whole cities were embodied on the stage. The perspective vista required frontal presentation, with the audience in a space facing the action. It promoted a sort of courtly hierarchy determined by who in the audience might sit closest to the duke, whose position in the center back of the house corresponded to the ideal viewpoint for the false perspective. The further the spectator sat away from the duke, the more flawed the false perspective. Ultimately, it meant the creation of an actual window, the proscenium arch, through which the audience viewed these rich, deep vistas. The proscenium arch enabled a variety of scenes and machines to create ever fresh visions.

In essence, the difference between these two models of the Renaissance theatre lies in the Elizabethan tendency to expand beyond the playhouse's confines, allowing the stage to engage multiple locales, versus the Italian tendency to contain its world within the proscenium,

presenting to the audience the illusion of a specific place. It led Eliza-
bethan playwrights to an expansive, comprehensive dramaturgy and the
Italians to a concentrated, contained play structure. This distinction was
much less sharp at the outset. The perspective cityscapes in palace halls
or courtyards functioned like a mansion—standing behind the action
and indicating emblematically a place. The same phenomenon held true
in such permanent theatres as the Teatro Olimpico in Vincenza and
the Teatro all'Antica in Sabbioneta. Then, the proscenium arch became
the standard feature, permitting changeable scenery. Soon after the turn
of the seventeenth century, the Italian theatre evolved in a direction
far removed from the Elizabethan, or, for that matter, the Spanish or
French. When the Italian theatre began to include the public by incor-
porating the box-pit-and-gallery configuration, the so-called Italianate
theatre emerged. Within a few years, by 1650, the Italianate theatre
had become the standard for all of Europe.

This long and exhilarating journey—from the first staging of ancient
plays, to new plays staged in the ancient manner, to the first playhouses
—culminated in the triumph of the Italianate theatre. The different
configurations created a vibrancy of spatial relationships between spec-
tator and spectacle and between actual and virtual activity that makes
the reemergence of the theatre building in the Renaissance a particu-
larly fascinating moment in the history of theatre.

## Work Cited

Wilder, Thornton. 1961. "Some Thoughts on Playwriting." *Playwrights on
    Playwriting*, ed. Toby Cole. New York: Hill and Wang.

# The Social Evolution of

# Shakespeare's Globe

## Andrew Gurr

THIS SHORT HISTORY is a new (coat of) gloss on a long period of rapid change that is misleadingly called evolutionary. Yet, that is still the most shapely metaphor to cover the multitude of influences that shape the end product, which is generally thought of as a new birth. The antecedents of Shakespeare's Globe are complex, a set of trends that often bore little connection to one another before they converged on London's Bankside in 1599. When Richard Dutton says the London playhouses were too "mongrel in their pedigree" to be copies of the classical Vitruvian playhouse, he offers a metaphor that suits a shorter timescale than this forty years, 1559 to 1599 (41). It is not so much the breeding as the slower adaptation to the changing ecological niches that I would like to emphasize. Since there is a real question about how much control any one person could have exercised over the frenetic changes happening in London at this time, evolution is the best word for it.

First, for all the magical aura that surrounds the Globe because of Shakespeare's involvement with it, we ought to register its second-best character in the eyes of its builders in 1599 and then its extraordinary success thereafter with those same builders, the players who owned it. That success is the first thing to register. It was built as a cobbled-together replacement for the two playhouses the company had recently lost. James Burbage's aging open-air playhouse, ambitiously named the "Theatre" when he built it in 1576, was designated as the company's home by the Privy Council in 1594. They lost it when its lease expired in April 1597. By then Burbage had built as its replacement a new indoor playhouse in a great hall in the Blackfriars. He tore down the partitioned tenements at considerable cost to build a whole new theatre.

Yet, the local residents, who included both the Lord Chamberlain, Cobham, and the company's new patron, George Carey, the new Lord Hunsdon, objected to the idea of the crowds and the noise of drum and trumpet that a playhouse would bring. Their petition to block it was upheld by the Privy Council (on which of course the Lord Chamberlain served). So the years from 1597 to 1599 were a bad time for the company. Building the Globe was forced on them by the loss of the Blackfriars, their intended replacement, and the site owner's ban on their reusing the old Theatre.

In the end an ad hoc consortium of the Burbage family and the player-sharers, composing a remarkably antimonarchic cooperative in an authoritarian age, put together what was left of their money after the Blackfriars fiasco and hired a builder, Peter Street, to demolish the Theatre and take its framing timbers as the basis for the Globe. This was a desperate and, in the strictest terms, an illegal act, since by common law buildings on leasehold land reverted to the owner when the lease expired. The site owner, Giles Allen, charged Peter Street with trespass and the Burbages with the theft of £800 worth of building timbers. The consortium fought him off over the next two years, but it cannot have been exactly the triumphant act of invention that the Globe is usually taken to be.

As an act of commercial collaboration and collective capitalism it was a new start because 50 percent of the cost was put up not by the Burbage sons but by five of the sharers, including Shakespeare. The consortium of playhouse owners also formed a majority in the company that was the playhouse's tenant. The tenants became the majority shareholders in the property they rented. This accidental innovation arose from the extreme conditions of the time, made necessary by the fact that most of the Burbage capital was encumbered in the Blackfriars. Yet, it was so practically and effectively expedient that it lasted the company and its playhouses for the next forty-three years and was probably the main foundation for the company's continuing success. In the entrepreneurial monopolism of Tudor commerce it was a notable anomaly.

And it was a remarkable triumph. The success of the Globe was partly the cause and effect of this commercial, expedient merger of playhouse landlord and tenant. The company liked the new relationship, as did the theatre owners. That is clear from what happened in 1608 when the Burbages got their Blackfriars theatre back. It had opened in 1599 with a boy company, which cancelled its lease during the plague closure of August 1608, returning possession to its original heirs. What the Burbages then did shows the high value they and the company now put on the Globe, their nine-year-old open-air theatre. They could have moved to the Blackfriars as James Burbage had planned in 1596, and rented the Globe to another company. Or they could have rented the Blackfriars. Instead, they chose the extravagant path of using both playhouses themselves for the one company.

There were reasons for this decision that go some way back in the evolution of the London playhouses, reasons that I will address later. The 1608 decision entailed a renewal of the Globe deal, with half the playing company's sharers becoming "householders"—co-owners of the second playhouse along with the first. It was a sacrifice for the Burbages, who could have kept it for themselves and rented it out very profitably to a rival company. It was extravagant because if one company was to use both places it meant leaving one of the two playhouses constantly empty and unprofitable. In the years that followed, six companies in London were chasing five playhouses, two of which were in the hands of Shakespeare's company, leaving a net shortage of two London theatres. That the Globe continued as one-half of this costly deal was strong testimony to how much the company had come to like it.

This affection was put to the test in 1613, when the Globe burned down. The fire required them to use the Blackfriars for most of the next year while the Globe was being rebuilt. This alternative, smaller Blackfriars with its much more wealthy clientele soon proved itself to be more profitable than the Globe. Yet, the controlling half of the company, which had shares in the two playhouses, still chose to dig into its pockets and rebuild the Globe. They built it more expensively than ever, and quite unnecessarily. In doing so, the owners paid the second of two tributes to the Globe's charisma, each of them shelling out hundreds of pounds to get it back. Exactly why they did so is a matter we can only speculate over. Its charisma, the end product of its evolution, is not my subject here. How it evolved into its place—how it became the primary Shakespeare playhouse—is the more intricate and yet, perhaps, the more readily answered question. I have told much of this story before, but it forms a necessary preface to the story that follows.

The Globe was unique in three ways. It was the first London playhouse to be owned and built by the company that performed in it. As the first home-designed workplace for players in London, it gave them the security of expecting to perform there for at least the next thirty-five years. And it was owned by one of the only two companies to have Privy Council backing for their tenure in the London suburbs. The Council specified the Globe in its order of 22 June 1600 as the company's only fixed and licensed playhouse. The security that the Privy Council order gave to the company and its new playhouses is important, because it was almost unique. These unique features of the Globe represent the historical essence of London playing through the forty years up to 1599—the four decades that ended when the professional English traveling companies first established themselves with regular playing places in London.

In effect, until 1599, all the English companies were traveling groups. They included a visit to London as one part of their wide-ranging annual travels. Their plays were designed to be transported on wagons (with a few of the leading players on horseback) in a constant round of shifting from one town to another across the country.[1] Their venues ranged from scaffolds in marketplaces to the halls of great houses. In London, they performed at inns inside the city—to large numbers in the yards of the coaching inns and to smaller numbers in the main rooms during the winter. Until 1594, all companies, however long they worked in London, were travelers.

No new setup, especially in the theatre, can be ideal. The professional English companies would have rated the Globe at its inception as the second or third best of the various options for playing places. By 1599, they had acquired ample performance experience not only in open marketplaces but indoors, through occasional appearances at court and in the great halls of country houses as well as the guildhalls of just about every large town in the country. Forty years earlier, on 16 May 1559, a printed proclamation from the new queen had ordered all local justices and mayors to censor the traveling companies prior to their performances before an innocent population. Mayors and their corporations, having a proper sense of their own dignity, were never going to stand in a marketplace to view the visiting players. So these town leaders opened guildhalls, the biggest and best meeting rooms in town, for the players to perform in.

As the force of the 1559 proclamation died down, the queen's new Master of the Revels, appointed in 1578, took over the role of censor. Access to town halls was restricted more and more as the town corporations began to count the cost in broken windows, doors, and the indignity, as one town put it, of allowing a room designed for justice to be used for common entertainment.[2] The use of guildhalls for plays was banned in Norwich in 1589, Great Yarmouth in 1595, Durham in 1608, and Chester in 1614. At Bristol, an order in 1585 banning plays

---

[1]The many volumes of *Records of Early English Drama* provide a remarkable listing of company visits to towns and through counties in England. The records for the decades after 1559, when Elizabeth's proclamation required mayors to judge plays before they could be released to the community, show a remarkable growth in activity and a consistent pattern of touring along with the gradual constricting of expertise to a few major companies, for the government licensed only a few, each run by a senior noble acting as patron.

[2]I owe thanks for this evidence to the editors of *Records of Early English Drama*.

from the guildhall was sternly renewed eleven years later. But there was not much consistency in observance of this rule. The Bristol order of February 1596 said "there shall not be any players in interludes suffred at any tyme hereafter to play in the yeald hall of Bristoll beinge the place of Justice." Although it imposed a fine of £5 on future mayors who broke the ban (to be deducted from the mayoral fee of £40), Derby's Men appear in the records receiving thirty shillings that July, and the Queen's Men £2 in August, both for playing "in the Guildehalle." There is no indication that the guilty mayor lost his £5. Instead, the consequence was that the players performed in the large rooms of neighboring inns. At Bristol, York, and elsewhere, inns were converted into indoor playhouses. At Norwich, Oxford, and other places, inns became the standard venue. Sometimes the yard was used, but often plays were staged in the main upper room. The shift from marketplaces, where the players circulated through the crowd, hat in hand, to venues with strong doors where nobody got in until they had paid, did wonders for the finances of the traveling companies.

Most mayors throughout England, including London's Lord Mayor, were hostile to theatrical performances. The 1559 proclamation forced the mayors to view shows that they would have avoided if it had not been a part of their official duty. That duty did not apply to the successive Lord Mayors of London, who were not as constrained by the proclamation as their less urban equivalents in the country. In the city of London, the players never got into the Guildhall, although they had plenty of indoor venues open to them. Until 1594, when the Privy Council joined the Lord Mayor in banning all playing inside the city limits, they played in rooms indoors at inns such as the Bell or the Cross Keys, as well as in the open yards at the Bel Savage and the Bull. One of the unexplained surprises in the history of theatre structures during these years is that the professional players preferred open-air playhouses to the halls. While their country travels had made them more familiar with the halls, the companies opted for open-air venues in London. Several special factors are involved in this. From 1559, the provincial playhouses were indoor venues—only London had open amphitheatres. Lacking the benevolent climate that sponsored the Spanish *corral* theatres, in a tangible sense they were a retrograde step in the evolution of the playing places, at least in the experience of the players themselves. We ought to pause here to speculate—for there is only contextual evidence, and no direct testimony—about why this should be.

First, there is no doubt that the open-air playing places had a much greater audience capacity than enclosed inns. The Theatre of 1576, the Swan of 1595, and the Globe of 1599 all could squeeze in as many as three thousand customers. The Rose of 1587 could accommodate over two thousand spectators; 20 percent more after the enlargement of 1592. No indoor room could hold anything like that number. Even the custom-built second Blackfriars could take fewer than a thousand spectators, and probably, given that its audience was all seated, that figure was not more than six hundred. The chief feature that distinguished the Blackfriars auditorium from the Globe was that everyone had a seat. The standing-room audiences in the yard at the Globe could squeeze together much more tightly than the people sitting on the "degrees" in the galleries, adding nearly a third to audience capacity. Yet, it was an odd feature. The type of arena nearly equivalent to the amphitheatre playhouses, the bear- and bullbaiting rings, had no standing room because the yard was full of the animals. All customers for a baiting had seats in the galleries. The idea of customers standing in the yard was an old players' tradition, stemming from the long-running practice of setting up a scaffold in a marketplace. Nonetheless, it was a very important feature of the amphitheatres because it provided the opposite of what the indoor theatres offered: it gave closest access to the stage to those who paid the least.

Why did the open-air venue and standing around the stage become such a durable feature of the Globe and its fellow playhouses in London's climate? Audience size was one obvious factor, and better lighting than that available indoors was another. It was certainly not the superior income that came from the larger numbers, because the Blackfriars with its much higher admission prices produced nearly twice the Globe's cash. The strong tradition of marketplace staging that featured the energetic interplay and crosstalk between the traveling companies and their equally active audiences must have been a factor. There are many ways in which the Globe's daylight ambience is rooted in the staging traditions of the past. The Blackfriars was the future. The first step in this long process of change in Elizabethan staging had nothing to do with rethinking the plays. It was a matter of controlling audiences and their purses. This first step from the marketplace to the guildhalls, inns, and other ready-made buildings, including the amphitheatres, made it possible to restrict access to those who could pay.

The direct context for the next evolutionary step forward is material. The first durable suburban open-air playhouse, James Burbage's Theatre, built in the suburb of Shoreditch in 1576, was probably located there because of the persistent opposition of successive Lord Mayors to any playing inside the city. In London, the professional companies had been used to playing at city inns and elsewhere, although they knew the opposition at first hand. Burbage's decision to invest money in a purpose-built playhouse must have been based on the confidence he had acquired as the Earl of Leicester's servant and player in the previous few years. His brother-in-law, John Brayne, had built the Red Lion, a playhouse in Stepney, nine years before, and Brayne supported Burbage's new venture. More valuable as security, though, was the royal patent that Burbage had persuaded Leicester to obtain in 1574 that gave his company more authority than just their master's livery. That patent was helpful in the provincial towns but carried little weight in London. The Privy Council was tightening its control over playing, although they had not yet appointed an official, full-time controller. Burbage was pushy and saw a healthy and profitable future for the professional companies. However, London was still the most difficult place to perform in, so Burbage built in the suburbs just out of the Lord Mayor's reach.

The mid-1570s was a time of major developments. There was now some mileage in the special ability of the professional companies to provide royal entertainment for the Christmas season. A play taken "from the roads" was much cheaper to stage at court than a masque or children's show, although that point had not really impressed the Lord Chamberlain in the 1570s. The new Master of the Revels recognized only after 1578, when he first started toting up the annual accounts for the royal Christmas, that professional companies could stage plays at court for one-quarter the cost of a masque. Through the 1580s the traveling companies went from strength to strength with their ability to provide good entertainment at court at short notice and cheaply.

In the mid-1570s, though, before the Master took on his interventionist role, there was an extraordinary two-year flourish of theatre building in London. Burbage built his Theatre in 1576; a colleague built the Curtain, also in Shoreditch, in 1577; Burbage's rival, Jerome Savage, who led Leicester's brother's company, Warwick's, built the Newington Butts theatre, also in 1576; and two indoor playhouses, Farrant's first Blackfriars and the Paul's playhouse abutting the cathedral, the only theatre actually inside the ambit of the Lord Mayor, all sprang into life.

In this flurry of playhouse building there was undoubtedly a strong copycat element. Yet, this sudden flurry of investors' cash suggests that there was a series of new factors. The large innyard theatres like the Bel Savage were still available, and so were inns with indoor rooms inside the city. With two hall theatres appearing in 1575 and 1576, why did the professional companies put all their reliance on the open-air venues?

The easy answer to that is social—the English class system. Public performances of plays were still thought of, especially by the players, as marketplace affairs. Because they catered to large numbers, they needed outdoor venues. The indoor theatricals were for the court, nobles in great houses, the gentry of the Inns of Court, and the mayor and his fellow dignitaries in the guildhalls. The only radical development in the building of the Theatre and the Curtain was their fixity in the suburbs and the specialized function of the venue. The Bel Savage in the city could continue to serve beer when no players were in town. The Theatre by contrast was totally dependent on the companies who played there, and the companies were still entirely travelers. They would not expect an extended stay even at the custom-built playhouses, because a long stay in one place put very heavy demands on their repertory of new plays. The greatest and most protected company of the 1580s, the Queen's Men, is on record as playing at almost every single venue, inn, and playhouse then available in London. From 1585 to 1594 they played at the Theatre, the Curtain, and the Rose playhouses in the suburbs—some of which were also known as "liberties"—and at the Bel Savage, the Bull, and the Bell inns inside the city. In these years, the companies were still entirely travelers.

The name "Theatre" seems to indicate Burbage's ambition—and an exceptional one it was. In 1576, if you spoke of a "theatre" to educated people, they would probably assume you meant an atlas, a map of the world, a *theatrum mundi*. Mercator's atlas, first published in England in the 1590s, was called a *theatrum*. John Speed's *Theatrum imperii,* published in 1611, used the same name. Speed and Mercator had first use before the playhouses took the name over. By using an Anglicized form of the Latin name for his playhouse, Burbage must have been thinking in the language of the *imprese*—the iconic and cryptically signifying terms that provided the name that his son invented for the Theatre's successor. James Burbage's choice alluded to the wonders of Rome and to the glories of the world, just as the playhouses, holding their mirrors up to nature like the mapmakers, tried to depict them. If nothing else, it shows the high status of his ambition and his expectations about the place playgoing would occupy in London's society.

Even without the association to Atlas (the giant who held the celestial globe on his shoulders), an association which also had in it the embryo of the playhouse's second name, I am sure that Burbage regarded the Theatre's name as a reference not only to maps of the world but also to Roman structures. Heywood, in his *Apology for Actors,* written a few years after the Globe was built, certainly made the connection when he said of Roman theatres that "every such was called *Circus,* the frame Globe-like and merely round" (D3v.). In 1596, the Dutch priest Johannes de Witt, who might have been expected to know his Vitruvius and the characteristic D-shape of the Roman theatres as distinct from the circuses and amphitheatres, made the same connection when he saw the Swan and the other London playhouses before the Globe was built.

London's journeyman playwright, Thomas Dekker, knew something of it too, since he mocked the post-Mercator pretension to "cast the Globe of . . . the old *théatre du monde . . .* into a new mould" in *The Gull's Hornbook* (7), published in 1609.[3]

At least in name, the Globe was a precise evolution from the Theatre. The same scaffolding made a *theatrum mundi* and a globe of the sublunary world. Yet, other steps in the evolutionary process between the Theatre of 1576 and the Globe of 1599 had to come first. The main step was taken by two privy councillors in 1594. Since 1584, the Lord Chamberlain Henry Carey and his son-in-law Charles Howard, the Lord Admiral, had taken responsibility for providing the annual court entertainments. The events of May 1594 saw the establishment of two approved companies, forming a duopoly that Carey and Howard set up to replace the original 1583 monopoly of the Queen's Men. For the councillors, this innovation guaranteed a supply of the queen's Christmas pleasures (Gurr 159–74). The Lord Admiral's and the Lord Chamberlain's Men were set up to replace the earlier Queen's Men, who after eleven years failed to do the job they were established for—providing the main features of the queen's annual Christmas entertainment. The Queen's Men had not staged a play at court since 29 December in the 1591–92 season. In the 1593–94 season, which had the smallest number of professional plays in a decade, the Queen's Men were brought back for one last play. It was evidently poor enough to prompt the Lord Chamberlain Carey and his ally, Lord Admiral Howard, to make a new start, this time with two companies instead of the original one. The queen's company kept its patent, but the two new companies under their own patrons had exclusive access to performing at court from 1594 to 1600.

The privy councillors gave them other backing too. They contracted with the Lord Mayor to ban all playing at the inns inside the city from then on, and they held to that policy, although Carey was persuaded to ask the city for leave for his company to play at the Cross Keys inn that first winter. That request may not have been granted, for Carey never asked again. The two suburban amphitheatres became the year-round venue for the two privileged companies. The Lord Admiral's group, formed around his long-time servant Edward Alleyn, was allocated the

---

[3]Dekker mocked the Globe's name rather than its claim to a Roman antecedent, but he fits it into an image of modern decay from the early models. Theatres are images of nature, but now "how wonderfully is the world altered, [having] lien [*sic*] sick almost five thousand years," so that the modern *theatre du monde* is utterly unlike its predecessors (Dutton 41). His French alludes to Mercator's "Theatre" as an atlas, and to the concept that gave the Globe its name.

Rose, owned by Alleyn's father-in-law. The Chamberlain's group, formed round Richard Burbage, was allocated the Theatre, owned by Burbage's father. One company got all Marlowe's plays, the other got all Shakespeare's.

The deal that Charles Howard and Henry Carey set up was reaffirmed in several Privy Council orders in the following years. The policy was laid down quite explicitly in the June order of 1600, after a Clerkenwell resident had complained to the council about the building of the Fortune. In it the Globe was named along with the Fortune as the fixed and approved location for the two protected companies. It was ostensibly an order "for the restrainte of the imoderate use and companye of playhowses and players." It says, in part,

> Whereas divers Complaintes have bin heretofore made unto the Lordes and others of hir Majesties privie Counsaile of the mainfold abuses and disorders that have growen and doe Continew by occasion of many howses erected & emploied in and aboute the Cittie of London for common Stage Plaies. And nowe verie latelie, by reason of some Complainte exhibited by sondrie persons against the buildinge of the like house in or nere Golding Lane by one Edward Allen, a servant of the right honorable the Lo: Admirall, the matter aswell in generalities touchinge all the said houses for Stage Plaies and the use of playenge, as in particular concerninge the said house now in hand to be builte in or neere Goldinge Lane, hath bin brought into question & Consultacion amonge their LL. Forasmuch as yt is manifestlie knowne and graunted that the multitude of the said houses and the misgoverment of them hath bin made and is dailie occasion of the idle riotous and dissolute livinge of great numbers of people, that leavinge all such honest and painefull Course of life, as they should followe, doe meete and assemble there, and of maine particular abuses and disorders that doe there uppon ensue. And yet neverthelesse yt is Considered that the use and exercise of such plaies, not being evill in yt self, may with a good order and moderacion be suffered in a well governed estate, and that hir Majestie beinge pleased at some times to take delighte and recreacion in the sight and hearinge of them, some order is fitt to be taken for the allowance and mainteinance of suche persons, as are thoughte meetest in that kinde to yeald hir Majestie recreacion and delight, & consequentlie of the howses that must serve for publique playenge to keepe them in exercise. To the end therefore, that bothe the greatest abuses of the plaies and plaienge houses maye be redressed, and the use and moderacion of them retained, The Lordes and the rest of hir Majesties privie Councell, withe one and full Consent, have ordered in manner and forme as followeth.
>
> First, that there shall bee about the Cittie two howses and noe more allowed to serve for the use of the Common Stage plaies, of the which howses one shalbe in Surrey in that place which is Commonlie called the banckside or there abouts, and the other in Midlesex. And foras muche

as there Lordshippes have bin enformed by Edmond Tylney Esquire, hir
Majesties servant and Master of the Revells, that the howse now in hand
to be builte by the said Edward Allen is not intended to encrease the
number of the Plaiehowses, but to be in steed of an other, namelie the
Curtaine, Which is either to be ruined and plucked downe or to be putt
to some other good use, as also that the scituation thereof is meete and
Convenient for that purpose. Yt is likewise ordered that the said howse
of Allen shall be allowed to be one of the two howses, and namelie for
the house to be alowed in Middlesex, soe as the house Called the Cur-
taine be (as yt is pretended) either ruinated or applied to some other
good use. And for the other allowed to be on Surrey side, whereas [there
Lordshipps are pleased to permitt] to the Companie of players that shall
plaie there to make there owne Choice which they will have, Choosinge
one of them and noe more, [And the said Companie of Plaiers, being
the Servantes of the L. Chamberlen, that are to plaie there have made
choise of the house called the Globe, yt is ordered that the said house
and none other shall be there allowed]. And especiallie yt is forbidden
that anie stage plaies shalbe plaied (as sometimes they have bin) in any
Common Inn for publique assemblie in or neare about the Cittie.
(Dasent 329–31)

This was a formidable endorsement. It echoed the terms of the deal
first conceived in 1583 and set up properly, with designated venues for
the approved companies, in 1594. Now the two new playhouses that
offered long-term tenure to their companies were specified. It is little
wonder that both companies staged plays celebrating the names of their
new playhouses, the Globe, as all the world's stage, and the (good)
Fortune. That was the first and to my knowledge the only time the
practice of hailing the venue's name has ever been followed in England.

The Globe was the first playhouse built in England to the orders and
roughly to the design (give or take the prior dictates of the Theatre's
framing timbers) of the playing company that owned and intended to
use it as their permanent home. Thanks in part to its sharer system and
to its resident poet, it proved remarkably successful. However, it came
nearer the end of an evolutionary line than the beginning. Shakespeare
has been remade in different forms and for different theatres ever since,
all too many of them claiming to be Globes.

## Works Cited

Dasent, J. R., ed. 1905. *Acts of the Privy Council of England*. Vol. 30. London:
Eyre & Spottiswoode.
Dekker, Thomas. *The Gull's Hornbook*. [1609]. 1969. Reprint, Scholar Press
Facsimile edition, Menston.

Dutton, Richard. 1989. "*Hamlet, An Apology for Actors,* and The Sign of the Globe." *Shakespeare Survey* 41:35–44.

Gurr, Andrew. 1993. "Three Reluctant Patrons and Early Shakespeare." *Shakespeare Quarterly* 44:159–74.

Heywood, Thomas. 1612. *An Apology for Actors.* N.p.

*Records of Early English Drama.* 1986–. Multiple vols. Toronto: University of Toronto Press.

# The Reemergence of the Playhouse

## in the Renaissance

### Spain, 1550–1750

#### John J. Allen

COMMERCIAL THEATRE in Renaissance Spain began with performances in city squares around the middle of the sixteenth century by people like Lope de Rueda, whom Cervantes recalled seeing during his boyhood. The physical arrangements for such performances are similar to the sort of outdoor platform stages that appear in drawings and engravings from all over western Europe at the time and to the stage that Callot remembered in 1621 from *commedia dell'arte* performances he had seen in Italy. These performances in public squares soon moved to a variety of innyards and hospital patios, exemplified by the drawings of arrangements in Guadalajara and Almagro that are included in my discussion of "The Spanish *Corrales de Comedias*" in *New Issues in the Reconstruction of Shakespeare's Theatre* (Hildy). Equally varied purpose-built playhouses began to appear at least as early as 1574, when the Corral de las Atarazanas was built in Seville by the Italian architect, Diego Marín (Hildy 212). By the turn of the century, playhouses were being built all over the peninsula, with major theatrical activity in Madrid, Seville, and Valencia. From the 1570s, coincident with the arrival of the first *commedia dell'arte* troupes in Spain (most notably the company of Alberto Naselli, called "Ganassa") the Eucharistic plays performed on carts for Corpus Christi employed staging arrangements that soon appeared in the commercial *corrales de comedias*.

Jean Sentaurens has published a graphic re-creation of the three-cart *auto sacramental* staging arrangement that became standard in Seville after 1609 (Sentaurens 1984, 2:349). The tiring-room arrangements of these carts necessitated the construction of buildings, mountains, or some sort of elevation at each side to conceal them. Something similar must have been necessary, if on a smaller scale, in earlier days when only a single cart was used. As Sentaurens records, in 1560 Juan de Figueroa decorated the cart for *El triunfo de la iglesia* in Seville with "buildings and a mountain made of 16 yards of sewn cloth [16 varas de angeo, hilo y agujas, para el monte]" (Sentaurens 1984, 1:165–66). The position of the two carts—expanded to four in Madrid in the middle of the seventeenth century—varied somewhat and could be quite elaborate and spectacular (see fig. 1).

It seems clear that platforms, analogous to the two carts drawn up at either end of a third cart (or at the sides of a temporary stage set up in a town square), were provided in the Madrid *corrales*. These platforms were used for bench seating for spectators at *capa y espada* performances and for the more elaborate staging need for the common mountain or two-mountain scene. In other playhouses, such as the Corral de la Monteri in Seville, arrangements existed for the temporary erection of such platforms. This use of platforms is one of the distinctive elements that characterize the early Spanish playhouses as compared with their contemporary counterparts in London. Figure 2 represents my conception of the staging of Calderón's most famous play, *La vida es sueño*, showing how the lateral platforms in the Madrid *corrales*—evident by the 1580s—correspond in form and function to the three-unit staging of the *autos* for Corpus Christi (de Armas 36). This uniquely Spanish design represents a confluence in the 1570s of three

Fig. 1. The author's conception of the staging of the *auto sacramental* in 1635, by Pedro Calderón de la Barca, titled *El gran teatro del mundo* (John J. Allen)

Fig. 2. The author's conception of the staging of *La vida es sueño,* c. 1630, by Pedro Calderón de la Barca (John J. Allen)

elements: Spanish troupes acting in hospital patios and innyards, Italian *commedia dell'arte* companies performing in Spain, and the peculiar circumstances of the presentation of *autos sacramentales* at Corpus Christi. The result was a design so successful that it persisted virtually unchanged for a century and a half.

The tiring-house at the rear of the stage rose early in the seventeenth century to three levels. Each level contained three lateral divisions, for a total of nine niches available for multiple discoveries or use as balconies, city walls, and so forth. In addition, there was an attic for machinery above, the *desván de los tornos.* Lope de Vega likened this facade to a chest of drawers (Ruano and Allen 363), but it also looks quite like many Spanish altarpieces (*retablos*) of the period.

The ground plans of the two Madrid *corrales,* the Corral de la Cruz, built in 1579, and the Corral del Príncipe, which opened in 1583 (Ruano and Allen 41, 42), indicate little fundamental change over the long life of the theatres, except for one curious development: the position of the uprights that support the roof over the stage in the Cruz and the Príncipe. The posts in the Príncipe rise at the corners of the leading edge of the thrust stage, but those in the Cruz are set back,

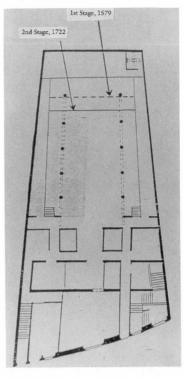

Fig. 3. Ground Plan of the Corral de la Cruz, 1785, showing the hypothetical original leading edge of the stage in 1579 and the leading edge of the modified stage in 1722 (John J. Allen)

quite like those in the well-known de Witt drawing of the Swan. This arrangement, however, does *not* seem to have characterized the original setup in the Corral de la Cruz.

The startling evidence presented by the discovery of the foundations of the Rose demonstrated how its original stage from 1587 had been modified in 1592. Suppose for a moment that the original Swan had a roof covering the entire stage, with uprights supporting it placed to each side of the leading edge of roof and stage. Then suppose that the stage floor was moved forward into the yard a few feet in an alteration similar to that of the Rose but in reverse, extending the stage further into the yard without moving the upright support posts. The result might resemble the de Witt drawing of the Swan. This change is in fact what happened, as indicated by repair documents, in the development of the Corral de la Cruz, built in 1579 and modified 143 years later by extending the stage further into the yard (fig. 3). I am not, of course, suggesting that this sort of modification produced this feature of the Swan design depicted by de Witt, only that the documentary evidence suggests this change actually happened at the Corral de la Cruz. The result is a curious similarity between the Cruz plan from 1735—the only *corral* ground plan that shows the roof support posts set back from the leading edge of the stage—and the design of the Swan (see Ruano and Allen 49–54). The extant *corral* evidence in Almagro and Alcalá de Henares indicates that neither theatre shares that feature with the modified Cruz.

The most peculiar and interesting feature of the two Madrid playhouses, and the one that was the most difficult to understand and reconstruct, is the lateral boxes for spectators. These boxes were rooms in neighboring houses, located outside the theatre proper, with windows and balconies opening onto the yard from each side; they simply hang in the air in my model of the Corral del Príncipe, depicted in figure 4, but they were of course entirely incorporated into the neighboring houses. A representation of the Corral de la Cruz in its Madrid city block (Ruano and Allen 133) indicates the different houses through which these boxes were accessed. The boxes were opened at different times over a period of several years, reaching a more or less definitive configuration by the time Lope de Vega died in 1635. This arrangement persisted throughout the life of the *corrales*. The control of spectators

Fig. 4. Model of the Corral del Príncipe, c. 1635 (John J. Allen)

that Burbage gained the day he opened the doors of the Theatre was not achieved by the managers of the Madrid playhouses until a century and a half later. In 1736, at the very end of the life of both theatres, new sets of boxes were constructed. These boxes, inside the lateral walls, blocked all of the former viewing spaces in neighboring houses.

What were the consequences of this peculiar arrangement for Spanish Golden Age theatre (cf. Ruano and Allen 182–96)? In *The Place of the Stage,* Steven Mullaney makes a convincing case for the importance of the location of Elizabethan playhouses (contemporary with the *corrales de comedias* in Spain). He contends that "when Burbage dislocated theater from the city, he established a social and cultural distance that would prove invaluable to the stagecraft of Marlowe and Shakespeare: a critical distance . . . that provided the stage with a culturally and ideologically removed vantage point from which it could reflect upon its own age with more freedom and license than had hitherto been possible" (130). He adds that "[t]he result is not so much a subversive drama as one rich in oblique commentary on its own times—on the relationships that prevailed between residual, emergent, and dominant values" (131).

What can be said of "the place of the stage" in Golden Age Spain— so similar in physical disposition to its Elizabethan counterparts—and of past relationships among poets, players, and the powers that be? In stark contrast to the situation so provocatively analyzed by Mullaney, the two Madrid *corrales* were placed in the very heart of the city. They operated under the direct control of the city council from the outset, and under the watchful eye of royal authority, too, in the person of the Protector of the Hospitals, a member of the Council of Castile who had authority to establish the regulations under which the theatres operated. The first two Madrid theatres, created by charitable brotherhoods to support their hospitals for the poor, were adaptations of existing buildings and the open courtyards (*corrales*) behind them. The brotherhoods were granted monopoly control, and commercial production of the plays was restricted to these two playhouses for over a century and a half.

Among the earliest boxholders were the most important people in the kingdom, all advisors and favorites of Philip III and IV: the dukes of Lerma and Uceda; Don Luis de Haro; and the infamous Rodrigo Calderón, marquis of Siete Iglesias. The list of boxholders in the decade from 1632 to 1642 includes four dukes, eight marquises, and twelve counts. The houses of people like Uceda, Lerma, and Rodrigo de Herrera, a knight of the Order of Santiago and Captain of the Guard in Lisbon, were described by a contemporary as "almost like royal residence" (Quintana, f. 376v).[1] Philip IV was an avid fan of the theatre and had a box in the Corral de la Cruz. The city also played an increasingly prominent role in the administration of the playhouses, taking over full and direct control of the operation in the 1630s. The city council had acquired its prominent box much earlier than that, sometime before 1602.

It seems, then, that conditions would certainly foster the servile, propagandistic theatre that a number of critics have detected in the repertoire of the *commedia nueva* of Lope de Vega and his successors. As José María Díez Borque has noted,

> from the beginnings of the 17th century, there is evidence of meticulous official intervention in the rules of operation of the Madrid theaters. . . . The Protector exercised complete authority, controlling the licensing of companies to perform in Madrid, permission to present a particular play after review and censorship, control of the accounts, approval of playhouse leases, and the naming of officials to police the theatres. A number of City officials also intervened in the control of performances. (21)

The economics of theatre during the period brought another significant element of control to the city to bear upon actors and playwrights: the extremely lucrative contracts between the city and the acting companies for the staging of processions and Eucharistic plays during Corpus Christi. The companies contracted to participate in the Corpus festivities in Madrid were well compensated. The contracts permitted the inclusion of a clause stipulating the exclusive rights of the company to produce plays in the theatres during the period between Easter and Corpus, a time of high attendance at the theatres. It also assured them of a number of contracts in nearby towns and villages. Moreover, selection to perform the Corpus Christi in the capital city conferred enormous prestige upon the company. Furthermore, the city contributed expense money, and, what may have been even more important, the company was able to completely renovate its wardrobe at city expense, since the Corpus costumes served perfectly well for the secular plays that the companies performed during the post-Corpus season (Calderón 20–21).

Yet, if this is the whole story, what about the comments of Cervantes, Lope, and other literary people, their constant complaints of the power of the rabble (*vulgo*) in the theatres? "Plays have become commercial

---

[1]This and subsequent translations are my own.

items," says Cervantes. "They are obviously nonsensical, but that's the way the *vulgo* wants them" (Cervantes, *Don Quijote,* 1:547, 545, respectively). "Since the *vulgo* pays for them," affirmed Lope de Vega in *El arte nuevo de hacer comedias,* "it's only right to talk down to them" (Rozas 182, ll. 47–48). At the end of the century, Bances Candamo could still complain that the dramatists followed, in their *comedias,* "the laws of the barbarous tastes of the people, accommodating them thus to make money for themselves or for the lessees of the theaters or for the acting companies" (52).

To begin to understand these comments, it is necessary to explore the process by which a play got produced in the Madrid of Cervantes and Lope de Vega, and then to take a closer look at the influences that were brought to bear upon the individuals who made the critical choices. The dramatist sold plays to the actor-manager of a company—the *autor,* as he was called—who, in turn, sold his repertoire and company to the lessee of the playhouses. The lessee contracted initially with the brotherhoods and later with the city. The lessee was a businessperson who had to turn a profit, and the manager had to make at least enough to keep his troupe alive and well. The commercial aspect of public theatre was particularly important in these early days of marginal economic advantages for those involved.

When an *autor* rented any of the available open yards in Madrid before the first permanent playhouse opened in 1579, he paid a flat fee to the owner for the use of the yard. Whatever he took in at the gate was his. This system was simply transferred to the Corral de la Cruz when it opened. In 1584, the general admission collected for the yard or the women's *cazuela* went to the actors, just as it had before. The brotherhoods received only the supplement paid to enter the stands at each side of the yard. At the same time, a small special collection for the hospital was established at the main entry to the yard, a collection that became standard and that was taken up at a "second door" to the yard. The distinction is important: everyone paid this charge as part of the general admission price. Perhaps five hundred groundlings, or *mosqueteros,* as they were called, remained in the yard and thus paid no supplement to the brotherhoods. The pricing arrangements for the stands and the benches used on them that began to be included early in the 1600s do not seem to have significantly increased the profits of the brotherhoods or the lessees who managed the theatres. Nor did this arrangement change the relative distribution of income among the actors and the various branches of management and control.

What can be said of the takings from the boxes—the money from the rich, noble families that first rented and then bought the neighboring houses where most of the boxes were located? The lessee could make something over 6,000 *maravedís* from the boxes, but it is important to note that half of that amount came from the lateral boxes, which generated money whether anyone was in them or not. The boxes were privately owned; annual fees were assured. The possible variation in the profits of the lessee was contingent on about 250 *vulgo* spectators, or about a third as much as the lessee stood to make from the stands and the women's *cazuela*. As for the actors, the equivalent of the money paid by sixty-nine *mosqueteros*, which the box income provided them, must have mattered very little in their considerations.

Although box prices were high, two considerations must have tended to nullify or at least mitigate the economic influence of the nobility and the upper classes on the *corral* playhouses of Madrid (I am saying nothing about the possible political or social influence of these groups; I am only considering profit and loss): the fact that very little of the profit from box receipts went to the actors, and the fact that almost all of the lateral boxes (located in privately owned houses) paid annually, whether they were occupied or not. Those house owners were not likely to sell the buildings if they didn't like a particular play or even a particular season of plays. As a matter of fact, these properties were regularly passed down from generation to generation within families later in the seventeenth century.

These circumstances are of capital importance to a consideration of Spanish Golden Age plays. An examination of the socioeconomic circumstances of theatre in Spain in the seventeenth century—without denying the complexity of the situation or the gaps in our knowledge—demonstrates a disproportionate influence of the two extremes of the social and economic scale. On the one hand, there was the control of the theatres by the brotherhoods, by the city, by the Council of Castile, and by the presence of powerful nobles in the boxes. On the other, the crucial importance of general admission receipts for financial survival gave considerable power to the people. Perhaps it is not so surprising that the typical Golden Age play seems somewhat schizophrenic: combining the exaltation of the faith and the monarchy in extraordinarily difficult passages of convoluted and conceit-ridden verse on the one hand with slapstick humor and provocatively sexy scenes on the other. The really good playwrights knew, as Cervantes and Lope insist, that they had to please the *vulgo* to get on the stage. Yet, they were aware that their plays were addressing some of the most powerful individuals in the kingdom, an audience to be flattered, cajoled, criticized, or remonstrated with, as they wished or dared. The "place of the stage" in the seventeenth century was, perhaps, a good deal more problematic in Madrid than in Mullaney's London.

I want to close with a very brief indication of how the Madrid *cor-*

*rales de comedias* were transformed into modern theatres, the eighteenth-century *coliseos* that replaced them. The incorporation of the lateral boxes into the playhouses was accomplished in 1736, as I have noted, and it was done as a temporary arrangement for special operatic productions in both Madrid *corrales,* but then only for a two-week period. It seems to have been a pilot effort to determine whether the constant problems between the lessees and the powerful families who owned the neighboring houses could be solved by simply walling them up. Later that same year the Corral de la Cruz was demolished and replaced by a fully self-contained *coliseo* playhouse. The demise of the Corral del Príncipe followed in 1745, replaced by a similar new playhouse. These new theatres featured the Italianate perspective stages that had been used in palace productions in Madrid for over a century, since the inauguration of the Coliseo del Buen Retiro in 1640 (cf. Dowling). A feature of the stage of the Coliseo de la Cruz in 1785 was that spectators in what had been the yard of the old *corral* were still standing, since the stage was about six feet high, as it was two hundred years earlier. The boxes facing the stage in the Coliseo de la Cruz were persistent design features of the old *corrales.*

Figure 5 depicts the arrangement of boxes and doors facing the stage in the Corral del Príncipe by the 1630s: two *aloxero* boxes to each side of a central entrance to the yard, initially introduced as refreshment stands but converted for spectators in the early evolution of the *corrales;*

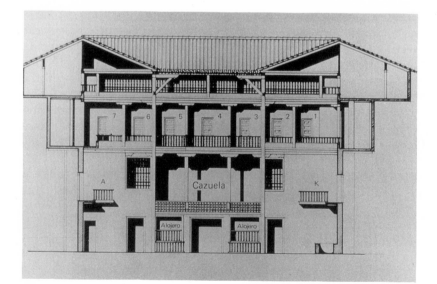

Fig. 5. Boxes Facing the Stage in the Corral del Príncipe, early 1600s (John J. Allen)

the women's *cazuela* above; and the *tertulia* at the top that seated those less austere members of the religious establishment who frequented the theatre. To each side, and not shown on this section drawing, were lateral *bancos de barandillas*—the degree seating on benches that characterized the *corral* design from its earliest days. The same features in the Coliseo de la Cruz reveal how these elements were integrated into the new design: two *aloxero* boxes to each side of a central entrance; the women's *cazuela* above them; the *tertulia* at the top; and to each side, the degree seating of the lateral *bancos de barandillas*.

One final illustration (fig. 6) shows how the *cazuela* design persisted in the wonderful Teatro Cervantes in Alcalá de Henares referenced earlier through all of its incarnations down to the movie theater that closed its doors in 1975. The *cazuela* drops slightly from the level of the other boxes in the second-level row and thrusts forward slightly into the yard, thus preserving these distinctive features of the original Madrid design copied from the Corral de la Cruz. The uprights supporting the *cazuela* define the position of the walls of the *aloxero*'s refreshment stands that characterized the *corral* built there in 1602, mute testimony to its forgotten origins almost four centuries ago.

Fig. 6. Central Boxes Facing the Stage in the Teatro Cervantes, Alcalá de Henares (John J. Allen)

# Works Cited

Bances Candamo, Francisco Antonio. 1971. *Theatro de los theatros de los passados y presentes siglos.* Ed. Duncan Moir. London: Tamesis.

Calderón de la Barca, Pedro. 1981. *El gran teatro del mundo.* Ed. Ynduráin, Domingo. Madrid: Alhambra.

Cervantes Saavedra, Miguel de. [1605] 1977. *Don Quijote de la Mancha.* Vol. 1, ed. John J. Allen. Madrid: Cátedra.

de Armas, Frederick, ed. 1993. *The Prince in the Tower: Perceptions of* La vida es sueño. Lewisburg: Associated University Presses of America.

Díez Borque, José María. 1988. *El teatro en el siglo XVII.* Madrid: Taurus.

Hildy, Franklin, ed. 1990. *New Issues in the Reconstruction of Shakespeare's Theatre.* New York: Peter Lang.

Mullaney, Steven. 1988. *The Place of the Stage: License, Play, and Power in Renaissance England.* Chicago: University of Chicago Press.

Quintana, Jerónimo de. 1929. *Historia de la antiguedad, nobleza y grandeza de la villa de Madrid.* Madrid: Consejo Superior de Investigaciones Científicas.

Rozas, Juan Manuel. 1976. *Significado y doctrina del'arte nuevo de Lope de Vega.* Madrid: Sociedad General Española de Librería.

Ruano de la Haza, Joséa María, and John J. Allen. 1994. *Los teatros comerciales del siglo XVII y la escenificación de la comedia.* Madrid: Castalia.

Sentaurens, Jean. 1984. *Seville et le théatre: de la fin du moyen Age a la fin du XVIIe siecle.* 2 vols. Bordeaux: Presses Universitaires.

———. 1991. "Los corrales de comedias de Sevilla." *Cuadernos de teatro clásico* 6:69–89.

Shergold, Norman D. 1967. *A History of the Spanish Stage.* Oxford: Clarendon.

# Historicizing the Sixteenth-Century Playhouse

## Ronald Vince

THIS PAPER CONCERNS certain issues of scholarly method and procedure arising from the study of sixteenth-century playhouses. A recurrent and inevitable pattern is the oscillation of scholarly attention between data and hypothesis, evidence and theory, the specific and the general: the hermeneutic circle, if you will, that allows us to make meaningful statements about both the Teatro Olimpico and Renaissance architecture, about both the Globe playhouse and the Elizabethan theatre. The process also illustrates the seeming paradox that history, though held by Aristotle to be less philosophical than poetry because of its particularity, actually gains strength as it abandons the particular and approaches theoretical abstraction. Claude Lévi-Strauss conceives of this paradox in terms of an information-comprehension dyad: "The historian's relative choice is always confined to the choice between history which teaches us more and explains less, and history which explains more and teaches less" (262).

Clearly, not every historian would agree with Lévi-Strauss. Those adhering to "nuts and bolts" theatre history and those who engage in theoretical speculation are likely to remain distrustful of each other. Nevertheless, the disagreement is more apparent than real: data has no significance, or even existence, without a contextualizing hypothesis, and theory is pure fiction without data (although fiction can have a potent persuasive power, especially if masquerading as history). Also related to the hermeneutic circle is the bicamerality of historical discourse—the double view of the past through the lenses of both the past and the present (Vince 23–25). As we move from the contemporaneous to the contemporary, we also tend to move from the particular to the general, from information to comprehension, from fact to theory.

A corollary to these observations is the axiom that historical scholarship is itself historically determined. We are all ultimately confined by our own cultural and institutional constructions. Breakouts occur rather less frequently than popular conceptions of rapid change imply. There are always strong forces—cultural, intellectual, social, political, economic, institutional—calling us back to orthodoxy. The tensions between orthodoxy and potentially disruptive challenge nevertheless help to define scholarly discourse and, together with the ever changing hermeneutic circle, underlie the creation and dissolution of scholarly paradigms. And historiographical paradigms, it seems to me, are not so much displaced by more powerful theories as they become victims of their own inertia: they are replaced not because they fail to answer questions adequately but because they continue to provide answers to questions that are no longer asked.

As far as sixteenth-century playhouses are concerned, then, there are two possible points of entry into any discussion. On the one hand, we can examine how these structures have been historicized—that is, the way that they have been featured in general historical discourse. Several pertinent questions arise: How are these structures related to earlier and later performance spaces? How do they relate to one another? How do they relate to the period that seems to contain them? What part do they play in the historicizing both of the period and of performance? On the other hand, we can examine the details of individual playhouses, their immediate purposes, their size, their shape, the interior configuration of their auditoriums, stages, and *frons scenae*. How did they function as performance spaces? The questions that begin with size, shape, and configuration, however, inevitably move toward the more general point of entry. What theatrical design or conception informed the details of construction? What economic, political, social, or aesthetic causes contributed to their erection? Why were they built where they were built? What was their relationship to their architectural and geographic surroundings? How did they function in terms of the larger culture? How were they interpreted, not only by the audiences that attended them but by society in general? How were they interpreted symbolically? What do they symbolize for the historian? What meaning do they have for the society of which the historian is necessarily a part? Why, in April 1995, are we here in Athens, Georgia, talking about sixteenth-century playhouses?

I propose to begin with the more general entry point suggested by the title of this conference: "The Reemergence of the Theatre Building in the Renaissance." Implicit in the title is a narrative that historicizes sixteenth-century playhouses as resurrections in a new key of classical structures, continuing the story of such structures that had been so unhappily interrupted by the fall of Rome. In this discourse, Renaissance theatre buildings were conceived, designed, and erected on the basis of a revived classicism derived from Vitruvius and traceable in the work of Serlio, Palladio, Scamozzi, and Aleotti. This work is viewed as experimental because these architects were attempting to reconcile Vitruvius's hints about the tragic, comic, and satyric scenes with his description of the architectural facade that would somehow enclose these scenes. Serlio, seeing the problem as a matter of choice between *frons scenae* and scene (conceived as wings painted in perspective rather that as *periaktoi*), opted for the perspective scene. The Vitruvian facade disappeared, as did the possibility of rapid scene changes. The architectural centerpiece of this narrative, the Teatro Olimpico, offered a compromise. Palladio provided a version of the Vitruvian facade that was pierced by five arches. Scamozzi placed a Serlian perspective scene behind each opening. The inevitable next step, it is held, was taken by Scamozzi at Sabbioneta, where he enlarged the central opening in the *frons scenae,* transforming it into a proscenium arch that framed a full Serlian perspective scene. When the Teatro Farnese, designed by Aleotti, with its picture-frame opening, deep scenic stage, and horseshoe-shaped auditorium, was built in 1618, not only was the baroque theatre finally in place but so were architectural principles that were to dominate European theatre architecture for the next two hundred years.

As we shall see, this narrative is not altogether satisfactory, but it does fit wonderfully with a common paradigm for Western theatre history. This model locates the origin of theatre in ancient Greece, traces its decline in Republican Rome to its death in the final years of the Roman Empire, points to its rebirth in sixteenth-century Italy, examines the emergence of a new classicism in seventeenth- and eighteenth-century Europe, and rejoices in the culmination of the tradition in the realistic-naturalistic theatre of the twentieth century. Thus Vitruvius and Serlio are to theatre architecture what Aristotle and Castelvetro are to dramatic theory. Since legitimate theatre requires both purpose-built playing places and dramatic texts, medieval performance—which appears to have lacked both—can safely be omitted from the narrative. At the same time, structures that could lay no claim to a Vitruvian pedigree, representing dead-end evolutionary experiments, are marginalized or ignored. Only a few years ago, a scholar blandly referred to the Teatro Olimpico as "the first permanent theatre in continental Europe built especially for the performance of plays" (Oosting 1). This phraseology allows Elizabethan playhouses in by the back door, perhaps, but makes chopped liver of the Corral de la Cruz (1579) and, especially, the Hôtel de Bourgogne (1548). To the best of my knowledge, no one has been able to bring the Bourgogne within the Vitruvian vortex

(Lawrenson), but there have been several attempts to make something Vitruvian of Elizabethan playhouses (Campbell; Yates; Orrell 1983). Also, the notorious "inner stage" seems to have been initially invented to provide a sixteenth-century precedent for a seventeenth-century proscenium arch and thus to bring English theatrical architecture into the dominant narrative.

The neglect of a thousand years of theatrical performance and the marginalizing of the French, Spanish, and English playhouses reflect serious limitations in the Vitruvian narrative. An alternative to identifying the beginnings of the baroque theatre in the architectural experimentation of the sixteenth century is to treat sixteenth-century playhouses in terms of the medieval design traditions that informed them. The method here is comparative and therefore has the merit of trying to account for the variety of playing configurations and stage designs represented by buildings as disparate as the Olimpico, the Bourgogne, the Cruz, and the Globe. As George Kernodle notes, "We get the impression of unrestrained invention in all directions" (2). In his attempt to deal with this variety, Professor Kernodle sees a peculiarly Renaissance aesthetic problem being solved in different ways.

The medieval world had dealt with diversity and multiplicity, change and flux, by reading the world in terms of a divine plan. Medieval drama universalized time, collapsing past, present, and future into a single topological narrative; medieval staging, with the *decor simultane,* universalized and collapsed space. The development of perspective, both as a drawing technique and as a metaphor for unique human perception, made it necessary to redefine unity in human and individual terms. (It is no accident that the three unities feature so prominently in Renaissance and neoclassical dramatic theory.) Kernodle nevertheless focuses the issue relatively narrowly: "The greatest problem of the Renaissance stage was the organization of a number of divergent scenic elements into some principle of spatial unity" (7). He finds solutions to this problem in the traditions of medieval and Renaissance art. Renaissance stage and scene design did not derive from ancient practice and precept but "as an entirely logical development in the history of the visual arts—the realization in three dimensions of the forms and conventions of painting, sculpture, and the *tableaux vivant*" (Kernodle 216). What Kernodle believed he had found were medieval solutions to a Renaissance problem.

Although Kernodle found a Renaissance unity in the problem, the solutions he identified in a common artistic heritage fit rather neatly into two categories that correspond roughly with the privileged and marginalized theatrical structure of the Vitruvian narrative: the perspective or illusionistic stage of the academy and the court, and the symbolic scenic facade of the Elizabethan public playhouse and the

Spanish *corral*. There is, of course, a temptation to interpret these "courtly" and "popular" theatres in terms of a struggle for supremacy that culminated in the complete triumph in the seventeenth century of the perspective stage (Kernodle 201–2). This triumph was perhaps most fittingly symbolized in the Coliseo del Buen Retiro (cf. Dowling), a court theatre built in 1640 by Cosme Lotti but open to the public and designed to reproduce the playing conditions of the *corrales,* including audiences (McKendrick 226). The popular *corral* was metaphorically swallowed by the court theatre. In fact, metaphoric and symbolic readings of sixteenth-century playhouses, both in terms of their interior configurations and their geographical and topological locations, have in recent years replaced attempts to explain them in terms of chronological historical narrative, whether conceived as a sequence of cause and effect or as part of a given tradition.

For example, semiotic analysis is concerned with the theatre building not just as a performance space but as a structure conveying a wide range of social meanings. Such analysis involves "every distinct element of the theatre complex," considered both synchronically and diachronically (Carlson 8–9). Italian theatres, initially constructed within princely palaces, carried with them—in the perspective that defined and related stage, auditorium, and city—the principle of princely power and magnificence. Perspective "emphasized the order imposed upon space by the political master of that space, the centrality of that master's vision, and the increasing insignificance of objects as they were located at greater distance from the position of power" (Carlson 22). Commentators have provided similar readings of Elizabethan public playhouses, noting that their location on the margins of London symbolized their ambivalent position vis-à-vis the dominant power structure, both upholding and challenging orthodoxy. Steven Mullaney's concern is "to locate popular drama both culturally and topologically" (9), "to situate Elizabethan drama in the context of marginal spectacle," and to relate it to an "ambivalent tradition of cultural displacement and display" (25).

These theoretical constructs have considerable explanatory and persuasive power. It seems clear that the Renaissance theatre building, whether courtly or popular, both symbolized and exercised control—over playing space, actors, and audiences—for the purposes of political, social, or economic profit. Moreover, there were aesthetic and philosophical issues. The point of these structures was not so much to present a theatrical performance as to restrict it, to confine it. The medieval street theatre, universal in time and place, made a performance space of God's world and was in turn structured by God's world. Jacques's comment that "All the world's a stage" applies most appropriately to the medieval theatre, where God the Father structured the narrative and God the Son was the major player. But Jacques offered his comment in a playhouse that inverted the metaphor. He made his point on a restricted, elevated stage before a restricted, enclosed audience; the world was symbolized and restricted by the "Globe" playhouse (Stroup). Similarly, it can be argued that the perspective of the Serlian stage imposed order on medieval diversity, now reinterpreted as chaos. Renaissance playhouses, whether popular or courtly, contained and imaged the world. They can be read metaphorically as attempts to reimpose order on human experiences that persistently flout the divine order. Courtly theatres shift scenes in an attempt to capture a moment in time and space; characters on the public stages become living emblems valued for their abilities to transform and change. Both actor and playhouse in their self-conscious theatricality are "metatheatricalized," calling attention to the ephemeral, insubstantial nature of the controlling dramatic and theatrical constructs.

This is heady stuff. But many scholars who have concerned themselves with the subject have chosen to examine or to reconstruct specific playhouses—devoting far more attention to the details of their construction than to their social, political, or cultural meanings. The emphasis on local circumstances requires a different set of hypotheses to explain the various playhouses: (1) ad hocism, whereby the structure is determined strictly by local conditions and happenstance; (2) economic determinism, whereby the capacity and structure are determined by economic considerations; and (3) architectural creativity on the part of the builder. There is often a further assumption that there are larger principles in the background—aesthetic, performative, architectural, technical. Thus, the Teatro Olimpico has been explained in terms of Vitruvian planometrics, theatre archeology, Palladio's stylistics, and certain practical contingencies (Oosting); the Hôtel de Bourgogne by the nature of the previous playing spaces used by the Confrérie de la Passion and the size and shape of the available plot (Deierkauf-Holsboer); the Corral de la Cruz as an ad hoc structure "developed piecemeal over the years to satisfy the demand for revenue and changing audience conditions" (Orrell 1988, 12); and the Globe as the product of Elizabethan *ad quadratum* building methods (Orrell 1983). These explanations are put forward with varying degrees of conviction, and there is room not only for alternative hypotheses but for other analyses that try to explain the strikingly similar forms and functions produced by different design traditions.

For example, the different geneses of the Elizabethan playhouse and the Spanish *corral* cannot disguise the fact that, in their fundamental configurations and use, the two structures are similar if not identical (Allen 1983, 113–15; Allen 1990; McKendrick 184). John Allen suggests a possible historical explanation for the similarities, postulating a European tradition of theatre architecture deriving from the influence of peripatetic Italian designers (1983, 117; 1990, 212). Kernodle can argue that the Olimpico "might have been exactly the same if neither Vitruvius nor the ancient theatre had ever been discovered" (171), and Orrell (who finds a "careful Vitruvianism" in the Olimpico) can be equally certain that there exists no "specific link between the Globe's design and that of the antique theatre described by Vitruvius" (1983, 147). Yet, the formal similarities to Vitruvius in the Olimpico and the Globe continue to impose themselves. Attempts to explain these similarities take us further from the sticks and stones of specific playhouses to abstracted and philosophical principles of Humanist architecture, founded in Platonic metaphysics, Pythagorean mathematics, and musical harmonics. As Orrell notes, Renaissance design "takes its departure from theories about the ideal proportionality of the cosmos" (1988, xiv; Oosting 20),[1] and there are many points of contact between the Globe's design and that of Vitruvius's ancient theatre (Orrell 1983, 140). Ultimately, Orrell cannot resist a kind of neo-Vitruvian rhapsody, necessary, he says, "to rescue the Globe from the pale indeterminacy of a mere scaffold" (1983, 152). Sticks and stones are not enough. If hermeneutic oscillation has a final direction, it appears to be in the direction of theory.

The procedures and hypotheses I am sketching are the very stuff of scholarly discourse. The results are tentative, ambiguous, incomplete, indeterminate. In a world governed less by cause and effect than by chance and probability, there can be no possibility of a single, "correct" interpretation of evidence, or a single, "correct" approach to that evidence. Incomplete evidence is a defining condition of historiography. Postmodern theory has reversed the traditional impulse to find harmony in chaos and stresses instead the inevitable ambiguity beneath an imposed order (Vince 25).

Abstractions, however, are wont to founder on the exigencies and circumstances that impact human behavior and belief. Examples can be found in the attempts over the past 250 years to reconstruct—in verbal description, sketch, model, or actual building—some version of the Elizabethan playhouse. Edward Capell initiated the enterprise in 1767 on the grounds that the space in which drama was played was relevant to its understanding—an initially radical notion that is now a seemingly

---

[1]Both Orrell and Oosting point to Rudolph Wittkower's seminal *Architectural Principles in the Age of Humanism*, first published in 1949 but revised in 1952 and again in 1965.

uncontested tenet of orthodoxy. Nonetheless, the idea involves two quite different conceptions of dramatic text. For Capell, and many of his scholarly descendants, the physical circumstances for which a playwright initially wrote his plays directly affected the dramaturgy, and a knowledge of those circumstances aided in interpreting the written text. More recent critics are less convinced of the literary nature of the dramatic text and instead view the playing space as a constituent part of the performance text. Rather than privileging the initial playing space, they treat it simply as the first among many variables that inevitably inform drama as performance.

What is now most striking about this "radical" enterprise, however, is how little its procedures have changed in two hundred years. With the exception of the de Witt drawing of the Swan (discovered in 1888) and the partial foundations of the Rose and the Globe (discovered in 1989), the same evidence was available to Edmond Malone as to John Orrell. Interpretative methodologies have been refined, as various nineteenth-century assumptions were questioned or discarded and, as Andrew Gurr records, "the syncretic conjectures of writers such as J. Cranford Adams . . . and the elaborate hypotheses of Leslie Hotson" were destroyed (Gurr 1970, 177). But fundamental historiographical assumptions have not changed. There is an assumption of the primacy of data and the possibility of finding a final truth in that data. And there is the further assumption of the historian's objectivity in interpreting that data. Thus, Franklin Hildy's recourse to the metaphor of the puzzle to describe the reconstructionist enterprise: "It has been a daunting task hampered by disagreements about which pieces actually belong to the puzzle, how much forcing of the pieces is allowable to make them fit, and indeed, about how much of the puzzle needs to be completed before we have as much of the puzzle as we need" (2). Professor Hildy's positivist methodology, whose persuasive power rests on the adequacy of evidence and the rigor of analysis, serves a useful purpose, but it also has serious limitations.

Most important, contrary to the positivist assumption, new evidence does not necessarily confirm or deny a current theory. As Hildy himself admits, the discovery of the Swan drawing "cannot be said to have immediately supplanted the Fortune contract or to have revolutionized Shakespeare studies overnight" (9). Nor, I might add, did the discovery of the Rose and Globe foundations. New discoveries are normally either dismissed or somehow incorporated into the orthodox model (as Orrell did with the Rose foundations in 1990). Data can become relevant evidence only within the context of a theoretical construct. We are dealing with probability as a function of subjective belief, and the treatment of evidence by institutionalized scholarship is a more complex process than positivism admits. The following, I suggest, is a more accurate description of the process:

> 1) The probability of the acceptance of a given piece of evidence increases as it is found to be congruent with other pieces of evidence.
> 2) An emergent hypothesis or model will increase the probability of acceptance of evidence fitting the general pattern, but it will at the same time decrease the acceptability of evidence that does not fit.
> 3) The point in the modeling process at which a piece of evidence is introduced will have a strong bearing on the probability of its acceptance.
> 4) Probability—in the sense of intensity of belief—increases as the model strengthens, as it moves from hypothesis to theory to paradigm.

Theatre reconstructions are clearly probabilistic, dependent for their acceptability on the degree to which they are found satisfactory by a given investigator or scholarly community. This satisfaction is normally based on the neatness of the fit with larger hypothetical systems that are sometimes abstracted from the specific instances they are invoked to explain. This version of the hermeneutic circle works as long as it remains open. But the circle can close; when it does, the paradigm becomes dogma—its power to explain replaced by its power to impose meaning, its persuasive powers dependent more on authority than argument. Not only are awkward hypotheses ignored or discarded—on paradigmatic rather than logical grounds—but the questions that are asked and answered can be severely circumscribed. In his discussion of the Globe, for example, Orrell omits details of the stage, tiring-house, *frons scenae,* and heavens on the reasonable grounds that the available evidence does not provide any relevant information. He dismisses questions concerning such matters as "trivial" and poses as the only question a rebuilt Globe can answer: What does a play *sound* like in such a structure? (Orrell 1983, xiv, 140).

The closing of the positivist paradigm is most clearly illustrated in the process by which the new Globe is being erected. At conferences and meetings, in books and articles, an academic community has conspired in the name of an arcane scholarship to convince themselves and the world that it is both possible and desirable to construct an authentic Globe playhouse. Central to the project is this appeal to authenticity. In *Rebuilding Shakespeare's Globe,* Andrew Gurr and John Orrell point with traditional scholarly caution to the conjectural nature of the construction they describe—"It is simply the best-informed conjecture that the present state of our knowledge allows us to provide" (42)—but they then proceed to ignore the conjectural aspects of the reconstruction and by the end of their book are regularly appealing to the "prin-

ciple of authenticity" and the "principle of accurate historical recon-
struction" (163).

The appeal to authenticity is to a certain extent a rhetorical
smokescreen. Building theatres is expensive, and if civic, philanthropic,
and commercial interests are to be enlisted in aid of the project, schol-
arly doubts and ambiguities must be thrust aside. Gurr and Orrell speak
of "experiment," but experiment ceases when architectural drawings are
made and real construction begins. The appeal to authenticity tends to
be comfortably supported by a scholarly community that has taken on
many of the aspects of an organized religion, complete with prophets,
saints, heretics, and priests. Periodic synods have established the parame-
ters of orthodoxy and legitimized the enterprise.[2] From 1973 to 1987,
and in apparent emulation of the Jesus Seminars, a series of consul-
tations provided the basis for—in the words of Frank Hildy—"a Globe
reconstruction that reflected the best guesses of the most widely pub-
lished scholars in the field of Elizabethan playhouse studies" (29). Only
such an ordained priesthood, it appears, can bestow the blessing of
authenticity. Shrines to the faith can be found from Odessa, Texas, to
Ashland, Oregon, but the new Globe will be the ultimate temple. It
will literally solidify a hypothesis.

Under these circumstances, can there be surprise that such an impo-
sition might prove unsatisfactory to those scholars whose visions are
fragmented by postmodern lenses, whose deconstructive methodologies
seek to disclose the chaos beneath the veneer of harmony, whose inten-
sity of belief varies inversely with the concretization of hypothesis?
Glynne Wickham, hardly a radical, pointed in 1979 to our ignorance
concerning key aspects of the second Globe, an ignorance that has not
substantially changed with the passing of fifteen years and the shift of
attention to the first Globe; his warning about Detroit's Third Globe
is equally relevant to London's new Globe. The use of a reconstructed
Globe "in the name of research will serve to solidify in the minds of
future generations all the errors that we have guessed into the building
as images of truth" (Wickham 148).

The complex of motives behind the building of the new Globe—
commercial, scholarly, narrowly professional, even exploitive and imperi-
alistic—involves agendas and ideologies far beyond those publicly ex-
pressed by scholars and historians. When the history of the project is
written, I suspect that it will not be a history of scholarly enterprise. It

---

[2]Conventions and meetings devoted all or in part to the reconstruction of the Globe
(either the first or the second) have been held at Vancouver (1971), Detroit (1979),
Evanston (1984), and Athens (1990).

will instead be a history of the same amalgam of motives that produced theatre structures in the sixteenth century. The historicizing of the new Globe may well parallel the current historicizing of Renaissance playhouses by cultural materialists and semioticians. I submit that historical enlightenment is more likely to come from a comparative study of the processes of theatre construction than from experimental performances. Reconstructionism has had a long run. As a historical method, it has run out. By every indicator save one, the Globe project may prove to be a resounding success. The new Globe may well be a "goodly theatre." But neither project nor theatre is good history.

## Works Cited

Allen, John J. 1983. *The Reconstruction of a Spanish Golden Age Playhouse: El Corral del Principe, 1583–1844.* Gainesville: University Presses of Florida.

———. 1990. "The Spanish *Corrales de Comedias* and the London Playhouses and Stages." In *New Issues in the Reconstruction of Shakespeare's Theatre,* ed. Franklin J. Hildy. New York: Peter Lang.

Campbell, Lily B. 1923. *Scenes and Machines on the English Stage During the Renaissance: A Classic Revival.* Cambridge: Cambridge University Press.

Carlson, Marvin. 1989. *Places of Performance: The Semiotics of Theatre.* Ithaca: Cornell University Press.

Deierkauf-Holsboer, S. Wilma. 1968. *Le Théâtre de l'Hôtel de Bourgogne.* Vol. 1. Paris: Nizet.

Gurr, Andrew. 1970. *The Shakespearean Stage, 1574–1642.* Cambridge: Cambridge University Press.

Gurr, Andrew and John Orrell. 1989. *Rebuilding Shakespeare's Globe.* New York: Routledge.

Hildy, Franklin J. 1990. "Reconstructing Shakespeare's Theatre." In *New Issues in the Reconstruction of Shakespeare's Theatre,* ed. Franklin J. Hildy. New York: Peter Lang.

Kernodle, George R. 1944. *From Art to Theatre: Form and Convention in the Renaissance.* Chicago: University of Chicago Press.

Lawrenson, T. E. 1986. *The French Stage and Playhouse in the XVIIth Century: A Study in the Advent of the Italian Order.* New York: AMS Press.

Lévi-Strauss, Claude. 1966. *The Savage Mind.* Chicago: University of Chicago Press.

McKendrick, Melveena. 1989. *The Theatre in Spain, 1490–1700.* Cambridge: Cambridge University Press.

Mullaney, Steven. 1988. *The Place of the Stage.* Chicago: University of Chicago Press.

Oosting, J. Thomas. 1981. *Andrea Palladio's Teatro Olimpico.* Ann Arbor: UMI Research Press.

Orrell, John. 1983. *The Quest for Shakespeare's Globe.* Cambridge: Cambridge University Press.

————. 1988. *The Human Stage: English Theatre Design, 1567–1640.* Cambridge: Cambridge University Press.

Stroup, Thomas B. 1965. *Microcosmos: The Shape of the Elizabethan Play.* Lexington: University of Kentucky Press.

Vince, Ronald W. 1990. "Issues in Theatre Historiography." In *New Directions in Theatre Research,* ed. Willmar Sauter. Copenhagen: Munsgaard.

Wickham, Glynne. 1981. "The Stage and Its Surroundings." In *The Third Globe: Symposium for the Reconstruction of the Globe Playhouse, Wayne State University, 1979,* ed. C. Walter Hodges, S. Schoenbaum and Leonard Leone. Detroit: Wayne State University Press.

Yates, Frances A. 1969. *The Theatre of the World.* Chicago: University of Chicago Press.

# On the Rebirth of Theatre,

# or of the *Idea* of Theatre,

# in Humanistic Italy

Luigi Allegri
Translated by Stanley V. Longman

DURING THE MIDDLE AGES, theatre died, or so it is said. I believe it would be more apt to say that the *idea* of theatre died, suffocated by a Christian culture that had long waged a virulent ideological campaign against it, for reasons I have explored elsewhere (Allegri 1988). This is not to say that there were no theatrical forms. It does mean, though, that the idea of theatre had virtually vanished. The society no longer provided an ideological niche for theatre, and thus all awareness of theatre's appropriate mechanisms or devices evaporated. This held true up to that moment when three distinct roads, the minstrel, the religious, and the humanistic, came together to stimulate the exploration and rediscovery of theatricality. Once that happened, theatre again found its basis in the written word and in the culture. Consciousness of the very idea of theatre finally emerged.

The minstrel and religious paths, both of which lie beyond the scope of this paper, yielded their greatest fruits outside Italy. The humanistic, however, is predominantly an Italian phenomenon. The effort to create dramatic texts from classical models triggered this movement, for it inevitably entailed the recovery of the literary dimension of theatre. Paradoxically, this imitation of the ancients set out to be, and truly was, radically new. Worthy of note, although again not the focus of this paper, are such experiments in playwriting as Albertino Mussato's *Ecerinis* or Enea Silvio Piccolomini's *Chrysis,* or what is perhaps even more important in hindsight, the vernacular compositions of Angelo Poliziano, such as his *Tale of Orpheus*. These works not only illustrate the prevailing preoccupation with classical dramatic structure, themes, and even language, they also bespeak a desire to break with contemporary theatrical practices that were so very distant from the classical, whether associated with the declining minstrel performances or the triumphant modes of the *sacra rappresentazione.*

For our purposes, perhaps the most interesting facet of this development is the staging not so much of new plays as of classical plays, especially those of Terence, Plautus, and Seneca. Scholars have taken particular interest in Terence, whose work was valued, at least for its literary value, well back into medieval times. Late-fifteenth- and early-sixteenth-century illustrations included in new editions of Terence give some indication of the nature of these early productions. The frontispieces of these volumes appear to depict either humanistic conceptions of Roman production practices or new practices contributing to the rapid evolution of the Renaissance stage (Nicoll 82–84; Kernodle 160; Flemming 33–52; Lawrenson and Purkis 1–23; Rey-Flaud 85–97; Ruffini 40–44).

Even on this score, I shall limit myself only to certain matters, because going into detail would require discussing the influence of both court entertainments and philosophical and aesthetic concerns on the shaping of the new Renaissance stage. These matters must lie outside the purview of this study. The current strategy for interpreting these illustrations is in no small way mechanical. Indeed, wishful thinking has no doubt distorted these interpretations, for we would like the pictures to depict a moment of passage from the medieval practice of disparate mansions to the unified Renaissance stage incorporating the mansions into a coherent structure, such as a city arcade. In this view, the medieval mansions, which had been autonomous and practicable places lined up one after another, now became decorative elements consistently incorporated into a unified global image.

To be sure, we are hard pressed to resist the temptation of a vision that so neatly charts the evolutionary progression when all we actually know are the points of departure and arrival. Nevertheless, the historical reality is much less vivid and much more contradictory. The debate over the real nature of those illustrations is still ongoing. We have yet to ascertain whether they depict actual contemporary mises-en-scène or imagined reconstructions of ancient scenic practices. They could be a little of both. After all, we know very little about how the academies of the late-fifteenth century (such as Pomponio Leto's Roman Academy or those in Ferrara, Urbino, Mantua, or Milan) produced Terence, or for that matter the newly discovered plays of Plautus and the tragic writers. We do know that the plays were performed on raised platforms, that they used scenic machines, and that scenery was sometimes used, and sometimes not.[1] Our best sources are restricted to contemporary

---

[1]See the summary treatment of these aspects, with indications of the sources, in Doglio (1:401–4, 446–56) and, more generally, in the documentation reported in Stäuble

descriptions of court performances, such as those provided in the Ferrara diaries of Bernardino Zambotti, who makes ample reference to the settings simply because he took the cause of stage reform so seriously. For example, his description of the setting for a production of the Italian version of Plautus's *Menaechmi* in 1486 states that the setting was mounted "in a new courtyard of the ducal palace, upon a new platform, in the form of a city on an axis with painted houses" (Zambotti 729–30).

But as I said, we must stop at this threshold. Something else must claim our attention now. The medieval period passed on to the succeeding era a set of cultural models and concepts that strongly affected the Renaissance approach to classical theatre. As Franco Ruffini has so convincingly argued, the Terentian illustrations, taken generally to be humanistic models of the classical theatre, do not so much show misunderstanding of the original as a preview of the theatre to come, their discards and alterations not really errors but deliberate decisions (Ruffini 23–26, 60). In the case of the architect Filarete, Ruffini asserts that these models result more from applying an idea *to* theatre than from inventing an idea *of* theatre. The same principle applies generally to humanistic theatre.

Humanistic mise-en-scène practices show more affinity with medieval traditions than we might wish to acknowledge. Ironically, they are tied to that ecclesiastical culture from which humanism sought to distance itself. The humanistic world assumed a solidarity and consonance with the classical world and so it tended to see itself as an outside culture, jumping globally over medieval heritage. The fact is, nevertheless, that medieval culture is not an impenetrable wall interposed between the humanistic world and its classical roots. Medieval culture, instead, contained many points of infiltration, many half-hidden holes, so that it was something more of a spongelike diaphragm that absorbed a good many classical elements and consigned them in filtered form to the succeeding epoch.

This was the situation with the idea of theatre. Toward the end of the medieval period, during the fourteenth century, as awareness of the ancient world began to prompt thoughts of remaking the present-day world, some accommodation for the idea of theatre had to be found. That was an especially vexing problem in a society that, having adopted liturgical and sacred drama, could no longer sustain its abrogation of theatre. The evident inadequate nature and substantial falsity of the

---

(187–202) and Cruciani (1983, 184–88, 219–27), which deals specifically with Pomponio's *accademia*. The basis of the learned historical studies that led to the decisive turn toward reconstructing theatre after "centuries without theatre" is developed by Giorgio Padoan (337–38).

Terentian reconstructions should be examined not by setting them against the original model but by measuring them against the knowledge and patrimony of values the protohumanists inherited from medieval culture. The theoretical model that comes of this is essentially unified. It depends on the shared sources or visions of its time. A thing never directly experienced can only be reconstructed out of known and understood elements. This is not far from Borges's description of the difficulty Averroes encountered trying to make sense of the words designating theatre in a culture devoid of any such notion (Borges 91–101). The difference is that we are dealing with a situation in which the idea of theatre is not entirely absent but appears only as a ghost bearing some seeming likenesses.

Strangely enough, some few scattered, yet more accurate, intuitive visions of the ancient theatre appeared in earlier centuries, in the eleventh century if not before.[2] These documents assume importance only in the perspective of the modern scholar seeking parallels and precedents; they cannot be seen as central to the culture of the time. It is only at that moment we are now examining, between the thirteenth and fourteenth centuries, that the reconstruction of the classical theatre takes focus in a cultural debate and begins to assume a life of its own. The effort is no longer episodic or sporadic but insistent, hastened on with multiple treatises. These treatises can be illuminating, particularly the commentaries on Roman dramatic works that were attracting more and more attention. A biographer of Terence writes:

> In each of Terence's comedies there are five acts, that is *recreationes* [pauses] that the comic author provided for a musical piece, the *neuma*, to be sung while the reciter rested and the mime artists, who had mimed the show in the 'proscenium' (that is, on the stall of the pulpit found in the theatre), entered into the conclave, which was called the scene, where the reciter had gone, and for the second time the mime artists changed costumes in order to perform another act or another scene. (Sabbadini 5:304)

The most striking image in this reconstruction is the split between the speaker of the text and the mute miming of the action, dividing the spoken word from gesture and business. Here one group, the mimes, takes responsibility for performance while a single individual, the poet, as it were, takes responsibility for the text. Medieval fantasy actually gave this figure an identity as a fixed character, Calliopius, who appears often in miniatures reading the text. Bizarre as this seems, it is

---

[2]A good example is the much-quoted passage of John of Salisbury (3:8) in which the metaphor of the world as theatre reappears.

natural to the culture of the time, which gave superiority to the voice—and even more to the written word—over any other communicative device. This corresponds with what Zumthor writes about the general relationship between the oral and written word in medieval culture:

> When the poet or his interpreter sang or recited (depending on whether the text is improvised or memorized), only the voice confers real authority. Tradition had granted prestige to the action of the voice. Should the poet or the reciter read from a book what the listener hears, authority emanates out of that book, a visible sign perceived as at the center of the entire performance. (Zumthor 1984, 335)

The presence of the book, then, was taken as a sign and source of undisputed authority, reinforced in no small way by the deliberate split between poet and actor. Indeed, this same split is confirmed in several diverse reconstructions of the ancient theatre. They remain quite consistent on this score up to the middle of the fourteenth century, and one can even find proponents of it in the late-fifteenth century.[3] An early example appears at the turn of the thirteenth century in the *Magnae Derivationes* of Uguccione da Pisa, where he speaks of *personae larvatae* (masked persons) who hid behind the scene and "at the sound of the reciter's voice appeared executing movements" (Drumbl 327). Perhaps the most important of these hypothetical reconstructions is Nicola Trevet's, dating from the end of the fourteenth century, for he possessed a widespread reputation as an authority on classical drama, especially on Seneca's work. We find this description in his commentary on Seneca's *Hercules furens:*

> Tragedies and comedies used to be presented in the following manner: The theatre was a semicircular area, in the middle of which was a small house called the scene. In this house was a pulpit. The poet ascended into the pulpit and there read his text at full voice. Meanwhile outside stood the actors, whose job it was to reproduce through gestures and business what the poet was speaking from the pulpit, each of them taking on a particular character. (Franceschini)[4]

An identical reconstruction, almost verbatim, using the same illustrative example (that of Juno calling on the Furies to torment Hercules),

---

[3]In *Politica litteraria* by Angelo Decembrio (1462) there is reference to an argument between learned gentlemen of Ferrara in which this reconstruction finds partial credit. On this score, see Stäuble (190–91). Less than twenty years earlier, Flavio Biondo in Rome reports an analogous formulation: see Cruciani (1983, 95).

[4]The Latin text is reproduced with commentary in the miniature of the *Codice Vaticano Urbinate* 355, with a visual representation of this arrangement on the reverse side of the first table printed in Franceschini.

is to be found some decades later in the commentary of Pietro Alighieri on his father's *The Divine Comedy*. There is, however, a slight alteration here. Trevet had spoken of *mimi* but here they are called "*mimi joculatores*," the term used to refer not to Roman actors but to medieval minstrels (Alighieri 8). This is a valuable piece of evidence, for it gives us clear indication that the minstrel tradition played into the reconstructions of the classical theatre, carrying with it the negative connotations associated with minstrelsy (Allegri 1988, 59–109). What seems to be happening in these endeavors is a reconstruction approximating an ancient prototype that had to rely on contemporary practices. This was virtually inevitable for a people attempting to conjure out of sparse evidence a theatre whose existence exerted suggestive power and yet lay beyond memory.

Medieval culture provided them three elements with which to complete the puzzle: the ancient dramatic texts, the minstrel tradition, and the memory of theatre filtered through Christian thought. All three of them together led to a necessary split between word and performance. Lacking any sense of ancient stage practice, the experience of the ancient texts was restricted to their literary values. In the eyes of medieval culture, the minstrel tradition was devoid of words, denigrated as dependent on mere gesture and business. And finally, the sole idea of theatre that endured through the ages preceding the medieval era appeared in the Christian encyclopedias derived from early sources that demonized the theatre and demanded action against classical culture.

In fact, this distinction between poet and actor, between word and gesture (always devaluing the latter terms, of course) appears in the works of two authors widely read in those centuries: Augustine and, especially, Isidore of Seville. The *Etymologies* of Isidore are probably the inspiration behind the views of Trevet and other fourteenth-century commentators. Augustine writes in the context of a discourse on the arbitrary nature and the codification of gesture: "If those signs made by dancing players had an innate sense by nature and not by rules and conventions among men in the earliest of times, then the gestures of the pantomimist would not require a speaker to explain to the Carthaginians what the dancer meant" (Augustine 60). Isidore writes in more detail on this same score:

> The scene was a place constructed within the theatre in the form of a house, with a pulpit that was called the orchestra where the comic and tragic actors sang or the players and mimes jumped about. . . . So the orchestra was the pulpit of the scene, where the dancer could perform or two people might argue between themselves. Indeed, the comic and tragic poets would join in the fray and while they sang the others acted. The mimes get their name from the Greek because they imitated human

action. In fact, there was an author who, before the mime performed, would tell the story. The poets actually composed the stories to lend themselves as much as possible to enactment with the body. (Isidore)[5]

Here we find those same misunderstandings that later show up in the biography of Terence, in Nicola Trevet, and in Pietro Alighieri. There is the scene that is like a house with a pulpit from which the poet spoke (though Isidore manages to confuse it with the orchestra). And there is that split between the word of the poet and the mute action of the actors. More important, though, is the fact that this distorted picture of the classical theatre, furnished by a seventh-century Christian, seemed entirely appropriate to the intellectuals of the fourteenth century to define an idea of theatre in keeping with their own age. The split between the poet's word and the actor's gesture, for example, is perfectly consistent with other attitudes of the times. The troubadours deliberately distanced themselves from the minstrels on the same principle. It is in accord with the long Christian moralistic tradition of the *turpis histrio* as performer of gesture and not of speech. Such attitudes would naturally prompt a reconstruction of theatre that claimed legitimacy by its inherent supremacy of word over action, of literature over acting.

However false it was historically, the recovery of a model of the ancient theatre emerged in good faith from the available facts. Moreover, at the time it served more as a projection into the future, a strategic move in response to a present undeniable need for theatre, than as an attempt at historical reconstruction. Or, to put it another way, the historical intent, certainly sincere over and above the misconceptions, favored a sort of cunning. We needed an idea of theatre, one that would be viable, credible, and unified. Given the scarcity of facts—not to mention the filtering those few facts endured as they passed down through various cultures—about an institution that had become a ghostly memory, such reconstructions are hardly surprising.

On a practical level, no doubt the model was never really operative, at least not in humanistic circles, and if it was ever realized, it would have been in connection with certain forms of religious drama, such as the *seinte resureccion* or the *semidramatic sermon,* which surely did not owe their structure to antiquarian purposes. Indeed, it is more than probable that this was a step backward in the sense that it served as a source for the late-medieval model (Rey-Flaud 20–36; Rousse 277–89).

Lacking documentation, one can surmise that the transition from

---

[5]This would seem to me to be the primary source, rather than that ever famous passage of Titus Livius (7:2) on Livius Andronicus to which Stäuble refers (188).

public reading of texts, a practice dating from Mussato's time forward, to fully staged plays at the various academies of the fifteenth and sixteenth centuries did not entail an intermediate step of public reading coupled with pantomime. Such an intermediate step was necessary only as an image in the movement toward the idea of a theatre. One could also surmise this because the reading-pantomime model had enjoyed some decades of circulation before its historical credibility was undermined. More direct evidence emerged, no longer mediated by the Christian tradition, of the real nature of classical culture. An indication of this is found in the fact that the two editions of Pietro Alighieri's *Commentarium* that followed the earlier edition containing the description inferred from Nicola Trevet contain no trace of such a reconstruction.[6]

This textual evidence suggests, then, that the reading-pantomime model was never part of the transitional passage. Beyond that, it was also a matter of practicality in the actual staging, as we witness in the illustrations that appeared just decades later in the editions of Terence's plays. If theatre could regain its legitimacy only by acknowledging the supremacy of the word—as evinced by the abundant publishing of new plays between the fourteenth and the fifteenth centuries, only a few of them actually performed—then it is also true that once theatre had been rediscovered or reestablished, it took off in the direction of visual spectacle. As I have written elsewhere (Allegri 1982, 133–45), if Renaissance society, for its own social and ideological reasons, invented a theatre that was radically new, artificial, and without roots, it could only do so if its audiences preferred watching over listening. This predilection shows up in the very first lines of one of the most important documents to give cultural definition to the new theatre, Poliziano's prologue for Plautus's *Menaechmi*, presented in 1488 in Florence: "Herein, we have been granted tongues as you have been granted eyes, for it is your part to watch and ours to speak and perform the play" (Poliziano 2:7, 282).

This formal separation of the watchers from the speakers and performers, in which the visual experience maintained a close rapport of all elements, was to lead to entirely new developments. We are speaking of the enormous alteration in the place and function of theatre in society. Theatre performed in the homes of the aristocracy, the rich bourgeoisie, or the landed gentry, and ultimately in the palaces of princes, is radically different than the medieval theatre performed in the churches and the city squares. Certainly some elements lend continuity between the sacred and especially farce traditions of the Middle Ages

---

[6]This appears in the *Commentarium*. For the dating of the versions, see "Analisi delle diverse redazioni," provided by the editors (xxi–xxv).

and the Renaissance or humanistic "regular" drama. The new elements, however, are infinitely greater: the deliberately literary structure; the return to classical themes in place of Christian ones; the creation of a spectacle intended for the privileged; the setting that provides an illusion of a unified world rather than a disparate emblematic staging; the adoption of frontal staging to aid the effects of false perspective; and the stratifying of the audience in the auditorium according to who is nearer or further from the eye of the Prince, the prime mover of the whole spectacle.

The fact that the setting is to be a unified vision watched from a singular viewpoint, namely that of the Prince, is related to a changing conception of space. Renaissance humanism, seeing space as measurable in human terms, played with it and took possession of it, making man the measure and center of the symbolic world and of the real space surrounding it. The same applied even to urban planning, for it also came out of a new model. This was a time of complete reorganization of the city layout. Drawing on Roman patterns, with straight lines providing perspective vistas and natural convergence on the center by regular avenues, the city became a unifying concept, bringing together the individual buildings into a single space, often in a scenographic manner. Indeed, the city became a stage set, and the stage setting became a city.

The greatest novelty of the Renaissance theatre lies in the structure of the stage set, which came to be called the *scena all'italiana* (setting in the Italian manner). This approach to staging, elaborated in the first decades of the sixteenth century, is fundamental to the idea of theatre that holds sway even today, creating a frontal vision that separates actors from spectators, the world of the play from the real world. With the *scena all'italiana,* the stage is no longer symbolic or allegorical of the world, as in medieval staging, but an actual model of the world, or at least of that concrete portion of the world we call the city.

Renaissance culture took primary interest in the stage set because the set provided both the basis for new images of power and the opportunity for new staging devices. The theatre building was of secondary and later interest, even if it, too, was a development of the Italian Renaissance. Throughout almost the entire sixteenth century, plays were performed in the large halls of palaces or in their courtyards, which were adapted as needed for each performance, or else they were performed in provisional free-standing theatre structures, such as the one built on the Campidoglio in Rome in 1513 on the occasion of conferring Roman citizenship on Giuliano and Lorenzo de' Medici (Cruciani). Not until near the end of the century did permanent theatre buildings go up. They include the two that gave an architectural basis for theatres of that age, two that we can even today visit and admire:

the Teatro Olimpico in Vicenza, planned by Andrea Palladio just before his death, begun in 1580, and inaugurated in 1585 with a performance of Sophocles' *Oedipus* Rex (Magagnato); and the Teatro Olimpico of Sabbioneta, built by Vincenzo Scamozzi, the same architect who finished the Vicenza theatre after Palladio's death (Mazzoni and Guaita).

These theatres evidently took inspiration from the theoretical writings of learned gentlemen and architects following the publication in 1486 of Vitruvius's *De Architectura*, the ancient Roman treatise that devoted ample space to describing the theatre of the time. In fact, the Olimpico of Vicenza was modeled closely on these classic originals, with a *cavea* describing a section of a circle and a stage decorated with a *frons scenae* in exact Roman style. The Sabbioneta theatre also employs curved, stepped seating topped by a loggia in the Roman manner, as does the much bigger Teatro Farnese in Parma, built in 1618 and inaugurated ten years later. This larger theatre is endowed with a spacious and deep stage area separated from the auditorium by a proscenium arch which concealed the scene machines that accommodated the elaborate baroque scenery (Cavicchi and Dall'Acqua; Ciancarelli).

By this time, the *scena all'italiana* had developed as an integral part of European stage practice. The necessity for a theatre building had emerged. Theatre had once again become part of our culture's heritage.

## Works Cited

Alighieri, Pietro. 1978. *Il* Commentarium *di Pietro Alighieri*. Ed. Roberto Della Vedova and Maria-Teresa Silvotti. Florence: Leo S. Olschki.

Allegri, Luigi. 1982. *Teatro, spazio, società*. Fosalto di Piave: Rebellato Editore.

———. 1988. *Teatro e spettacolo nel Medioevo*. Rome-Bari: Editore Laterza.

Augustine. 1962. *De doctrina christiana*. In *Corpus Christianorum Series Latina*, ed. I. Martin. Turnholti: Typographi Brepolis Editions Pontificii.

Borges, Jorge Luis. 1979. "La busca de Averroes." In *El Aleph*, 91–101. Buenos Aires: Emece Editores.

Cavicchi, Adriano, and Marzio Dall'Acqua. 1986. *Il Teatro Farnese di Parma*. Parma: Battei.

Ciancarelli, Roberto. 1987. *Il progetto di una festa barocca: alle origini del Teatro Farnese di Parma* (1618–1629). Rome: Bulzoni.

Cruciani, Fabrizio. 1968. *Il teatro del Campidoglio e le feste romane del 1513*. Milan: Il Polifilo.

———. 1983. *Teatro nel Rinascimento, Roma, 1450–1550*. Rome: Bulzoni.

Doglio, Federico. 1982. *Teatro in Europa*. 3 vols. Milan: Garzanti.

Drumbl, Johann. 1981. *Quem quaeritis: Teatro sacro dell'alto medioevo*. Rome: Bulzoni.

Flemming, Willi. 1960. "Formen der Humanistenbühne." In *Maske und Kothurn,* vol. 6, ed. Margret Dietrich, 33–52. Vienna: Institut für Theater Wissenschaft, Universtät Wien.

Franceschini, Ezio, ed. 1938. *Il commento di Nicola Trevet al Tieste di Seneca.* Milan.

Isidore of Seville. *Etymologiarum libri XVIII.* In *Patrologia Latina,* vol. 82, sections 43–49, columns 648–59.

John of Salisbury. 1993. *Policraticus.* Ed. K. S. B. Keats-Rohan. In *Corpus Cristianorum Continuato Mediaevalis,* series 118. Turnholti: Typographi Brepolis Editores Pontificii.

Kernodle, George. 1944. *From Art to Theatre.* Chicago: University of Chicago Press.

Lawrenson, Thomas E., and Helen Purkis. 1964. "Les editions illustrées de Térence dans l'histoire du théâtre." In *Le lieu théâtrale à la Renaissance,* ed. J. Jacquot, 1–23. Paris: Editions du Centre National de la Recherche Scientifique.

Magagnato, Liscisco. 1992. *Il Teatro Olimpico.* New edition. Ed. Lionello Puppi. Milan: Electa.

Mazzoni, Stefano, and O. Guaita. 1985. *Il teatro di Sabbioneta.* Florence: Leo S. Olschki

Nicoll, Allardyce. 1927. *The Development of the Theatre: A Study of Theatrical Art from the Beginning to the Present Day.* London: G. G. Harrap.

Padoan, Giorgio. 1973. "Il senso del teatro nei secoli senza teatro." In *Concetto, storia, miti e immagini del Medio Evo,* ed. V. Branca, 325–38. Florence: Sansoni.

Poliziano, Angelo. 1970. *Opera omnia.* Ed. Ida Maier. 3 vols. Torino: Bottega d'Erasmo.

Rey-Flaud, Henri. 1973. *Le cercle magique: Essai sur le théâtre en rond à la fin du Moyen Age.* Paris: Gallimard.

Rousse, M. 1987. "Aux sources de l'art de l'acteur médiéval." In *Teatro comico tra Medio Evo e Rinascimento: la farsa. Atti del Convegno di Roma del 1986,* 267–89. Viterbo.

Ruffini, Franco. 1983. *Teatri prima del teatro.* Rome.

Sabbadini, Remigio. 1897. "Biografi e commentatori di Terenzio." In *Studi italiani di filologia classica,* vol. 5. Florence: F. le Mounier.

Stäuble, Antonio. 1968. *La commedia umanistica del Quattrocento.* Florence: Instituto Nazionale di Studi sul Rinascimento.

Tissoni, Benvenuti A., and Maria Pia Mussini Sacchi, eds. 1983. *Teatro del Quattrocento: Le corti padane.* Turin: Unione Tipografico-Editrice Torinese.

Zambotti, Bernardino. [1486] 1983. *Diario ferrarese.* In *Rerum Italicarum Scriptores,* ed. Ludovico Antonio Muratori. Reprint, Città di Castello: Stamperia di S. Lapi.

Zumthor, Paul. 1972. "Jonglerie et langage." In *Poétique,* vol. 11, 321–36.

# "My Lord, the Parterre"

## Space, Society, and Symbol in the Seventeenth-Century French Theatre

### Virginia Scott

ALTHOUGH WE CAN identify many differences between the theatres of the Renaissance and baroque and our own, perhaps the most obvious difference—and one that characterized the theatres of England, Spain, and France—was the presence in the commercial theatres of the sixteenth and seventeenth centuries of a large standing audience, predominantly and usually exclusively male, closest to the stage and, indeed, forming a human barrier between the stage and the presumably more important audience in the galleries and boxes.

Unlike audience members of today, and unlike those who paid for a place to sit then, the men in the standing pit had freedom to move around, to find a better view, to greet a friend, to evade or confront an enemy, to buy a glass of lemonade in summer or a cup of chocolate in winter. Distractions were everywhere and our impression of the standing audience is that it was frequently, even continually, distracted and distracting. As with most elements of the early modern theatre, our usual point of reference is the theatre of seventeenth-century London; our impressions are formed by literary men and playwrights who apparently did not cherish the penny-paying "dullards" and "stinkards" who crowded round the stage. A "vulgar sort of Nut-crackers, that only come for sight," grumbles Jonson, while Shirley, as late as 1640, sneers at the "grave understanders" who delight in bawdry and ballads, shows, dances, and fighting (Gurr 1970, 153; 1987, 248–49).

The experience in France was somewhat different. In England, private theatres expelled the standing audience early in the century, while the larger and cheaper public theatres continued to welcome it until the interregnum. The presence of the standing audience in the one and its absence in the other marks an important distinction between the two kinds of performance space. In France, on the other hand, all theatres except the opera theatres retained the standing parterre until the eighteenth century.

Tracing the history of the parterre, both as a physical space within the theatre and as those audience members that peopled it, casts a certain amount of light on the way in which French professional theatre developed. Central and even essential early in the seventeenth century, the parterre was a subject of complaint and an object of contempt as the theatre was purged of farce and baroque elements in the late 1630s and the 1640s. Beginning in the 1660s, however, with a renewed emphasis on comedy, at least one French troupe embraced the standing audience, while the Italians, who became established in 1662 and were not obliged to pay any attention at all to the tenets of classicism, flattered and even eulogized what a character in the 1690s was to refer to as "*monseigneur le parterre*," my lord, the parterre (Gherardi 4:267). Throughout the century, perceptions and characterizations of the parterre are closely linked to repertory and especially to the decline and resurgence of farce.

Although development of the professional, commercial theatre was retarded in France in comparison to Italy, England, and Spain, France— or rather Paris—had the first known structure purpose-built for theatrical production in Europe. This was, of course, the celebrated Hôtel de Bourgogne, built in 1548 for the production of *mystères* by the Confrérie de la Passion. Although this building has been studied more thoroughly than any other French theatre, its original arrangements are not clear. Working backward from a remodeling done in 1647, various scholars have tried to reconstruct the primitive interior. However, aside from the overall dimensions of the space, and the depth of the stage and the number of boxes just preceding the remodeling, little about it can be said to be known with any certainty.

The salle (auditorium) of the Hôtel de Bourgogne in the first half of the seventeenth century was usually divided, in leases and other legal documents, into only three categories: the parterre (or *basse salle*), the loges, and the galleries, although a single mention in a lease of 1626 indicates that by then there was an amphitheatre at the rear of the parterre with a refreshment franchise, the Widow Dollin's two "little closets," beneath it (Fransen 348). The entry, the amphitheatre, the parterre, and the stage shared seventeen *toises*, or 108.7 feet, of length. The depth of the stage before 1647 was forty feet, leaving, let us say, nine feet for the entry, fifteen feet for the possible amphitheatre, and forty-five feet of open space for the parterre. The stage (and the parterre) occupied the total width of the building, which D. H. Roy has convincingly shown to have been seven *toises*, or just under forty-five feet (23). The parterre can thus be described as an open space on the ground floor, approximately forty-five feet square, which could hold an audience of about 500, giving each spectator a generous four square feet of standing room. With some variations in dimensions, and a few modifications I will mention later, this description holds through the century.

Before 1630, the parterre was definitely the most important part of the salle as far as the professional troupes that rented the Hôtel de Bourgogne from the Confrérie were concerned. Admission prices were set in 1609 (or 1619) at five *sous* for standing room and ten *sous* for a seat (Lough 14). There is no way to estimate the possible income from the amphitheatre and galleries, but we know that the theatre had only twelve loges, each holding at most eight spectators. We also know that the Confrérie retained the rights to five of the loges and that as many as four others were variously claimed. Assuming a full house, a troupe might take in 125 livres from the parterre and a mere 12 livres from the loges. Thus, we can conjecture that the repertory of the early professional theatre in Paris was largely meant to attract the parterre audience.

Unfortunately, nothing can be said with any security about the composition of the parterre audience of the Hôtel de Bourgogne in the early years of the century; there is an "almost complete absence" of useful information (Lough 13). What descriptions we have of the spectators, most of which are similar to descriptions of the groundlings in the English public theatres, are not, to my mind, reliable, since they originate in the 1630s and 1640s when the now genteel and refined theatre was trying to disassociate itself from its rambunctious ancestor. Many scholars have simply presumed, based on their own notions of propriety and morality, that because the entertainments provided by the professional actors at the Hôtel de Bourgogne before 1630 were sometimes crude and even obscene, the spectators attracted to them must have been drawn from the lowest levels of society. But this seems a dangerous assumption about the era of Henri IV, not the most refined of monarchs, and even the early years of Louis XIII, whose chief delight was the farce of the *commedia dell'arte*.

What evidence we have of the behavior of the theatre audience in the first quarter of the century is drawn almost entirely from the prologues of the *farceur* Bruscambille, who may or may not have been the orator of a troupe that performed at the Hôtel de Bourgogne before and after 1610. Much of what Bruscambille had to say seems aimed at calming noisy and impatient spectators; for instance, he points out that the actors cannot begin while "one of you is coughing, another is spitting, another is breaking wind, another is laughing, and another is scratching his ass." The audience must remember that "the bed is for sleeping, the table is for drinking, the Hôtel de Bourgogne is for seeing and hearing, whether seated or standing, and without budging" (Wiley 212). This plea is addressed, however, to both standing and seated spectators, and does not necessarily characterize the parterre. In fact, aside from being relatively sure that women did not stand there (although even that can be challenged), we have no information that allows us to distinguish the parterre from the other segments of the audience.

The whole audience seems to have preferred farce to any other genre. The troupes that leased the Hôtel de Bourgogne were both French and Italian. The Italians played the improvised comedies we now call *commedia dell'arte*, a mixture of romantic and farcical elements, heavily flavored in the early seventeenth century with pastoral fantasy and other baroque seasonings. French troupes like that of Valleran le Conte, for example, played a more extensive repertory—tragedy, tragicomedy, comedy, pastoral—but always with the addition of a farce. Thomas Platter tells us in 1599 that every day after the noon meal there was a play in French verse followed by a farce that "they performed so well, in unrhymed verse or in prose, embellishing it with such jokes and buffoonery, that one cannot keep from laughing"(Jomaron 117).[1] Actors had two stage names, one for the regular repertory, one for farce. Robert Guérin, for instance, played as La Fleur in the mainpiece and Gros-Guillaume in the farce. It was Gros-Guillaume and his colleagues in farce Gautier-Garguille and Turlupin who were able after 1615 to make enough money at the Hôtel de Bourgogne—in spite of the greed of the Confrérie—to stay in Paris for long periods of time and begin the process that led to an established theatre.

After 1629, and under the aegis of Richelieu, who was interested in developing a drama that would be classical, regular, and French, the troupe led by Guérin was granted a permanent lease on the Hôtel de Bourgogne, and a second troupe led by two successful provincial actors, Le Noir and Montdory, settled into a remodeled tennis court in the Marais. A number of young French poets began to write for the theatre: Mairet, Rotrou, and most notably Pierre Corneille. The last play that featured the three great farceurs was produced in 1633, the year of the death of Gautier-Garguille. Gros-Guillaume died a year later. Farce, the genre that had created the established theatre, was now to be excluded from it.

Knowing so little about the composition of the audience before 1630, we cannot offer any specific suggestions about how it changed

---

[1]This translation and all those that follow are my own.

after establishment. We can, however, notice that the audience is no longer spoken of as a unit. The parterre is now an entitity distinct from the loges, the amphitheatre, the galleries. This separation of the parterre may be partly the result of a physical change in the theatres.

At the Hôtel de Bourgogne, the parterre abutted a stage that was, according to Deierkauf-Holsboer, only about three feet high (1968–1970, 1:19). The parterre audience could stand, but it could also sit at its ease. In a lease from 1621, the actors are enjoined from interfering with the right of the Widow Dollin to place twelve stools in the parterre but are themselves also granted the right to put stools and benches wherever they like (Deierkauf-Holsboer 1968–1970, 1: 199). When the parterre was crowded, only those in front would be able to sit and see, and the others would crowd the stage and interfere with the view of those few spectators in the boxes. However, in the provinces, the ambulatory troupes were accustomed to converting nontheatrical spaces into theatres. Over half of the known provincial venues were tennis courts (Mongrédien and Robert 309–26), and it was the converted tennis court theatre, the Théâtre du Marais, not the old Hôtel de Bourgogne *mystère* stage that became the model for the Paris theatre.

A touring company adapted a tennis court into a theatre by installing in it one of the high trestle stages used in the outdoor farce and charlatan performances of the late Middle Ages. Any number of paintings and prints show us a simple platform, at head height, backed by a curtain and faced by a standing audience. At first, the actors simply recreated this arrangement indoors, and the audience remained in its familiar relationship to the stage. A few spectators—women, perhaps, or local dignitaries—would sit in one of the side or end galleries that made up part of the configuration of the tennis court, but the standing audience was the primary audience.

In the fully converted tennis court, however, the arrangement of the audience and the relative importance of its various segments changed. We can begin to describe the Paris theatres with some accuracy in the 1640s. The Théâtre du Marais, which opened in 1634, burned and was rebuilt in 1644. Sufficient documents survive to permit a reconstruction. We also know a good deal about the conversions of the two tennis courts occupied by the ill-fated Illustre Théâtre in 1644 and 1645. Finally, of course, we have the contract between the Confrérie and the carpenters who remodeled the Hôtel de Bourgogne in 1647.

What these theatres did was essentially overlook the parterre, in more ways than one. Providing comfortable spaces for higher-paying spectators and, especially, for women was now a priority. The repertory had been refined, purged of the farce that many now claimed had kept women out of the theatre before 1630. The stages both at the new Théâtre du Marais and at the remodeled Hôtel de Bourgogne were six feet high at the front and raked up toward the rear. The lower boxes were seven feet off the floor of the parterre, giving those who sat in them a chance to "overlook" the standees below who no longer interfered with the boxes' view of the stage or of each other. (Deierkauf-Holsboer 1954, 1:194–95; 1970, 2:183–85). The parterre had become a true pit, a sea of headtops easy to ignore, to overlook in the other sense.

The parterre audience simply mattered less in this new configuration. The Hôtel de Bourgogne went from a single row of twelve boxes to two rows of nineteen boxes each; the Marais had two rows of eighteen. At mid-century a full parterre at the Théâtre du Marais might have brought the actors 450 livres, but thirty-six boxes, each with eight seats at 2 to 3 livres a seat, was potentially worth 720 livres. The power structure within the audience had changed.

The parterre having become such a clearly distinct physical space, it should be possible to describe its occupants, and, indeed, a number of descriptions do exist. A common thread in the theatrical writings of the 1630s and 1640s is the assertion that the parterre is still filled with lower-class men expecting lewd and obscene farce. Georges de Scudéry is perhaps the most extreme in his characterization of "that animal with so many heads and so many opinions that one calls the *people*, . . . the ignorant multitude that farce attracts to the theatre, '*mezo huomo, mezo capra, et tuto bestia,*' as the Italians say" (Lough 65). In fact, by the late 1630s many other references indicate that the parterre audience was largely bourgeois; indeed, the theatre audience is often characterized by the opposition of "noble" to "bourgeois," as in Loret's remark that Magnon's *Zénobie* was played a second time "for the noble and for the bourgeois" (Lough 84).

By the 1640s the *honnêtes gens*, the decent folk who stood in the parterre, were certainly men of the middle class. The price of a place in the parterre had tripled. It now cost fifteen sous to see an ordinary performance, thirty to see a new play. Scudéry's "animals" could scarcely have afforded this on any regular basis.

Roland Mousnier has published widely his findings on social stratification in Paris in the seventeenth century. Based on marriage contracts and inventories after death, these studies propose to define nine social strata that represent the top 75 percent of the Parisian population. The first three include nobles of the sword, gentlemen, and nobles of the robe. The fourth is made up of lawyers, men who preface "*maître*" before their names. The fifth, sixth, and seventh strata include businessmen, merchants, and masters of the various crafts. The eighth stratum consists of *compagnons* or journeymen, the ninth of working men and servants (Mousnier 1976, 25–40). When members of the top three strata went to the theatre they undoubtedly sat in the loges or amphitheatre; members of the two bottom strata may have occasionally attended a performance and stood in the parterre; but I suggest that the majority of the parterre audience consisted of the middle sort: advocates and prosecutors, bureaucrats, merchants and masters.

Although Mousnier's analyses both of dowries and estates indicate that most of the members of the middle strata were literate (Mousnier 97–100), critics and writers did not find the parterre to have high standards. In a period when Chapelain, the abbé d'Aubignac, the abbé de Pure and others were trying to establish norms for the composition and judgment of plays, the tastes of the parterre were at best an inconvenience, at worst an obstacle. Farce aside, the favorite play of the bourgeoisie was *Le Cid,* and the *Cid* controversy was, I believe, in part a result of efforts by aristocrats like Georges de Scudéry to gentrify the French theatre and to discount the parterre audience. The abbé d'Aubignac wanted to change the parterre into the equivalent of our modern orchestra, with risers and individual chairs (Aubignac 176). This innovation would have created comfortable seating with a good view of the stage, for which the troupes would have charged higher prices, thus excluding many middle-class audience members. No doubt this is exactly what the abbé d'Aubignac had in mind.

Maurice Descotes writes in 1964 that by 1656 the new audience was supreme. "The fashionable people, the women, and the learned," he tells us, "had not chased away the popular public from the theatres, but they had imposed upon them their taste and the canons of their aesthetic" (91). According to the abbé de Pure, this state of affairs largely resulted from the influence of the fashionable women. "Women take part in judging everything. They know Euripides as well as they know Malherbe. There is scarcely a salon in Paris where lessons are not given on the unity of time" (Descotes 96). For Descotes and other modern upholders of French *classicisme,* the post-Fronde theatre had finally and successfully purged itself of popular and baroque inclinations and was ready for the cultivated and restrained tragedies of Racine. However, I think this point of view has been exaggerated.

French scholarly blinders have kept French scholarly attention fixed on the Comédiens du Roi at the Hôtel de Bourgogne and their repertory. The Théâtre du Marais, from the mid-1630s to the mid-1650s, appealed to bourgeois taste with the Roman plays of Pierre Corneille, the sanitized farces performed by Jodelet, and a series of machine plays. It is true that this theatre fell on hard times in the 1650s, and perhaps their "old-fashioned" repertory contributed to their problems. Still, the actors seem to have believed that they could resolve their difficulties with a reprise of Pierre Corneille's machine play, *Andromède,* and with new plays by Thomas Corneille who wrote, according to the abbé d'Aubignac, "fraudulent stuff for the bourgeoisie" (Lough 84).

Clear evidence of the importance of the parterre audience is the action taken in 1660 by the troupe of Molière and Madeleine Béjart. First established in 1658 in the grande salle of the Petit-Bourbon, a royal theatre used for ballets and Italian operas, the troupe was displaced when the Petit-Bourbon was demolished to make way for the new east front of the Louvre. Louis XIV then gave the actors permission to play in the grande salle of Palais-Royal, a theatre built by Le Mercier for Cardinal Richelieu in 1641. This theatre did not have a parterre; instead the space on the ground floor not occupied by the stage contained twenty-seven stone steps that, according to Sauval, rose "gradually and imperceptibly" to a height of thirteen feet. Benches were placed on these steps, with the result that "when the auditorium [was] full, one [saw] only heads, arranged in rows, one above the other" (Sauval 2:162).

What Palais-Royal had in 1660 was more or less what the abbé d'Aubignac had asked for, a raked parterre with fixed seating. What Molière and his troupe did, however, was refashion the space into a standing parterre, not flat but still slightly raked (Scott 91–93), an innovation that was duplicated by the Comédie-Française when it built a new theatre in 1689.

A place once provided for them, the parterre audience was praised by Molière a few years later in *La Critique de l'École des femmes*. The Marquis grumbles that *L'École des femmes* is detestable if for no other reason than the fact that it inspires continual bursts of laughter from the parterre. Dorante, the voice of reason, counters:

> You are then, Marquis, one of those fine gentlemen who grants the parterre no common sense, and who disdains to laugh with it, even at the funniest thing in the world. The other day, I saw on the stage one of our friends who made himself ridiculous doing just that. He listened to the whole play with the deepest gravity; when anything amused the rest of us, he merely scowled. At every burst of laughter, he shrugged and looked with pity at the parterre and sometimes he said scornfully "laugh on, parterre! Laugh on!" It was a second performance, the peevishness of our friend. . . . You must learn, Marquis, and the rest of you as well, that half a louis d'or does not guarantee better taste than a fifteen-sou coin; and that a misjudgment can be given standing or seated. Finally, all things considered, I am proud of the approval of the parterre, because some among them are quite capable of judging a play according to the rules and the others of judging it the best possible way which is to let oneself encounter things without blind prejudice, insincere praise, or ridiculous prudishness. (Molière 1:653–54)

The *Critique* is part of the quarrel of *L'École des femmes* that is part of the larger quarrel concerning what materials are appropriate for the stage. The critics, playwrights, and actors who had celebrated the triumph of refined tragedy were disconcerted by the reappearance of the old enemy, farce, and its popularity in the theatre of Molière. The modern reader is nonplused by negative reactions to *L'École des femmes* that seem out of proportion to the mild sexual equivocations present in the play. For the writers and actors of the rival troupe at the Hôtel de Bourgogne, however, this intrusion of bawdry into what was in other respects a well-made neoclassical comedy may have signaled the outbreak of a war they feared they could not win—a war over where the small Paris audience would spend its sous. In the *Critique* Molière makes it clear that the *sous* of the parterre are perfectly welcome at Palais-Royal.

Much serious study of the seventeenth-century French theatre ends after the 1670s. Molière died in 1673, and Racine retired from the commercial stage in 1677. For many scholars, the merger in 1680 of the two remaining French troupes into the Comédie-Française marks a convenient end date for *la classicisme*. Furthermore, a watershed in French culture was created by several nontheatrical events: the wars of 1672–78 and 1688–99 and the movement of the court to Versailles in 1682. The wars in particular led to a change in material circumstances responsible for significant social mutations. H. C. Lancaster writes that playwrights after 1680 were blessed with a whole new range of satirical targets, thanks to the wars, war profiteering, and the growth of the financial bureaucracy (1:5). What Lancaster does not explore in detail is the change in the theatre audience and the reascendency of the parterre.

With thousands of courtiers now in residence at Versailles or spending hours every day commuting from Versailles to Paris, with an ever-growing state bureaucracy, and with a large cohort of prosperous businessmen and merchants, the social fabric of Paris was transformed. Both at the Comédie-Française and its remaining rival the Comédie-Italienne, now playing at the Hôtel de Bourgogne, a parterre filled with powerful middle-class men was a force to be reckoned with. This ascendency of the middle class reflected the larger society, but it also came about because the parterre had discovered the power of the whistle. The men of the parterre agreed with Molière that they were persons of good judgment. They knew better than the exquisites on the stage or the savants in the amphitheatre or the ladies in the loges if a play deserved to survive. Those plays that did not deserve to survive were quickly whistled off the stage. Incidentally, the word *siffler*, which means in French "to hiss" as well as "to whistle," can refer to both behaviors, but by the late 1680s we can usually assume that the *siffleur* was blowing an actual whistle.

The power of the whistle is not at all the same thing as the power to withhold patronage if the play does not please. The action is aggressively rather than passively negative. Failure is immediate and brutal. The parterre's habit of whistling was no laughing matter for the actors, in spite of Colombine's claim in *La Descente de Mezzetin aux enfers* that they were actually enriched by it, that everyone came to the theatre on opening night for fear there would be no second performance (Gherardi 2:386). The acting troupes were constrained to cope with the problem, and their means of coping are significant.

The Comédie-Française, because of its adherence to genre norms, seems to have only occasionally tried to appeal directly to the better instincts of the parterre. Molière was bold enough to include in his comedies farce elements and such baroque idiosyncracies as metatheatricality and direct address, but his progeny were fainter of heart. They listened to Boileau, who refused to recognize the author of *The Misanthrope* in the pranks of Scapin.

Besides, the principal comic playwright of the Comédie-Française in the 1690s, the actor Dancourt, wrote for the taste of the upper classes (Lancaster 2:770), and the French continued their custom of doubling the admission price to the parterre for new plays. The Comédie-Italienne, on the other hand, took measures to make the parterre audience feel at home. They dropped the double admission price to the parterre for new plays, they produced plays designed to appeal to middle-class tastes and interests, and they made direct efforts in prologues and agons to cajole what was clearly a necessary element of their audience.

One of the earliest is the self-reflexive prologue to Regnard's *Le Divorce* in 1688. Jupiter descends from Mount Olympus expressly to see the play that, the actors tell him, has not been sufficiently rehearsed and is bound to be whistled off the stage. Jupiter points out that he has his thunderbolts with him and says that the first man to whistle will get his whiskers singed. Arlequin is appalled: "Oh, gently there, Monsieur Jupiter. Don't shock the parterre, please. We need it." He then begs the parterre to be charitable, and the play begins (Gherardi 2:110–11).

A more philosophical slant on the matter appears in Dufresny's *L'Opéra de Campagne* that opened in June 1692. While the opera is being prepared, Colombine and Arlequin debate the question: Is man a laughing animal or a whistling animal? Arlequin takes the question directly to the parterre: "You know, gentlemen, that it is very difficult to make you laugh; but nothing is easier than to make you whistle." The two end the scene with a wager. Arlequin bets the parterre will whistle, Colombine that it will laugh. "This is a sure way to see which of us is right," she says. "The thing most natural to man is whatever is hardest for him *not* to do. You beg these gentlemen to keep themselves from laughing during the whole comedy, and I will beg them to keep themselves from whistling" (Gherardi 4:4–8).

While the Italians sought to pacify the parterre—even proposing in the debate noted above that "it's the whistlers who shelter our stage from the deluge of bad writers who would flood us out"—the French literary establishment was distinctly unamused. Donneau de Visé's *Mercure galant,* on several occasions, pointed out that the best authors would not write for a theatre in thrall to a whistling parterre. "These sorts of people," Donneau writes, "only seek to amuse themselves at the expense of good sense and for the reason that they must want to get rid of all the plays. . . . I do not pretend, in condemning the whistlers, to defend all the plays that have been whistled, but neither should one conclude that all the plays that have been whistled are bad" (Mélèse 217). Bordelon writes a year or two later that apparently the whistlers wanted, even in first plays by new authors, heroes who spoke with the strength and the elevated tone of their long-time favorite, Pierre Corneille, and would mistreat any play that did not conform to this standard (Mélèse 218).

The Italians were more direct and perhaps more successful than the French in dealing with the problem of the whistlers. Their repertory was not open to comparisons with Corneille, for one thing, and they continued to play farces that permitted metatheatrical interpolations and direct address.

One final example will serve to show how the Italians blurred the distinctions between stage and audience and how far they went to welcome and even pander to the parterre. The play is *Les Chinois* by Regnard and Dufresny. The young heroine, Isabelle, is considering marriage with Octave, an actor at the Comédie-Italienne. She would like to be an actress, herself, and thinks she would please the audience. Octave has a rival, however, an actor from the Comédie-Française played by Arlequin. In the last scene of the play, Colombine, speaking for Octave, and Arlequin, speaking for himself, debate the relative merits of the French and Italian actors. As Isabelle's father prepares to decide which of the two should have his daughter, a preposterous figure enters, takes the father by the arms, and throws him to the floor. This is Le Parterre, played by Mezzetin dressed in a mélange of different fashions, with several heads, a large whistle at his side, and several others hanging from his belt. "How dare you," he says, "usurp my jurisdiction. I am the only natural judge, the Supreme Court of actors and plays." An armchair is brought and the French actor makes the error of inviting Le Parterre to sit, listen, and not interrupt with his whistle. Le Parterre pushes the armchair away: "You're joking, my friend, Le Parterre never sits. I am no ordinary judge, and I listen standing and never fall asleep at a hearing." Colombine, referring to French acting, says that this "imperial style, Roman attitude, and flashy sort of declamation might alarm me, if I were before a less enlightened judge than His Excellence, Monseigneur le Parterre." Arlequin foolishly objects: "Ha, ha, ha! His Excellence! Ah, there go the Italians, trying to flatter the listener in a prologue, and apologizing in advance to the parterre." Colombine responds: "I only render the homage due to this Plenipotentiary Sovereign. He is the spur of the playwrights, the check rein of the actors, the controller of the benches on the stage, the inspector and examiner of the high and low boxes, and all that happens within them; in a word, he is an incorruptible judge who, rather than taking money for judging, actually begins by giving it at the door."

After a long debate, Le Parterre gives his judgment. Since the Italians never charge more than fifteen sous and gave a free performance at the taking of Namur, he orders Isabelle to marry Octave. Arlequin appeals to the judgment of the boxes, but Le Parterre reminds him that *his* judgments cannot be appealed (Gherardi 4:263–78).

To actually bring the parterre onstage as a character is a bold move that deserves explication. Jeffrey Ravel, in a recent article, links Le Parterre of 1692, with his compound costume and multiple heads, to Georges de Scudéry's 1639 picture of the popular audience as a many-headed animal, the monster hydra that symbolizes the lowest ranks of the third estate in seventeenth-century antidemocratic political polemic (228). I have no doubt that this reading is accurate for Scudéry, whose goal was to purge the theatre of its popular elements, but I am less inclined to believe that Regnard and Dufresny are making the same symbolic statement in 1692, when the parterre was essential to financial survival and no longer made up of the lowest ranks of the *menu peuple* but of the solid middle class. Of course, the scene is not without satirical edge, but on the whole the writers and actors find the power of the parterre, My Lord the Parterre, appropriate and beneficial. It is Arlequin, speaking for the French actors, who calls upon the judgment of the boxes. It would be helpful if the stage direction described the costume of Le Parterre more fully, or if the frontispiece showed Mezzetin as Le Parterre instead of La Pagode. Given the information available, however, and looking at the context of the 1690s, my guess is that the character was meant to symbolize the various social categories that actually made up the parterre audience—the bureaucrat, the lawyer, the merchant, and the army officer—and to serve as a comic mirror in the baroque mode.

The comedies of the 1690s played by the Italians were not exclusively conceived for the parterre audience, but without the approbation of those middle-class men, success was improbable. They liked plays about themselves; they liked plays that satirized the war profiteers and other financiers. They enjoyed—and this is new—plays set in the country or in a village, at the grape harvest or the annual fair. They apparently did not object to the relaxation of manners that the stage mirrored, although they liked bourgeois characters who stepped out of line to get their comeuppance. They were fond of pretty girls, especially the outspoken and unconventional Colombine with her misanthropic edge. They liked to laugh. And as long as they were laughing, they weren't whistling. It was essentially a tired businessman's theatre, but nonetheless entertaining and full of life.

In the 1690s, the theatre had in some measure come round full circle. At the Hôtel de Bourgogne, where the Italians now played, the stage was higher than at the beginning of the century, and there was a small railed space for an orchestra at the center front of the parterre that had begun to interfere with the direct access of the parterre audience to the actors on stage. But the genre of farce still permitted Arlequin or Colombine, as it had Bruscambille eighty years earlier, to look the noisy, restless, but essential parterre in the eye, welcome him, scold him, and beg for his approbation. "De grace, Monseigneur Le Parterre."

## Works Cited

Aubignac, François Hédelin, abbé d'. 1968. *The Whole Art of the Stage.* New York: Benjamin Blom.

Deierkauf-Holsboer, S. Wilma. 1954. *Le Théâtre du Marais.* 2 vols. Paris: Librairie Nizet.

———. 1968–1970. *Le Théâtre de l'Hôtel de Bourgogne.* 2 vols. Paris: Éditions A.-G. Nizet.

Descotes, Maurice. 1964. *Le Public de théâtre et son histoire.* Paris: Presses Universitaires de France.

Fransen, J. 1927. "Documents inédits sur l'Hôtel de Bourgogne." *Revue d'Historie littéraire de la France* 34:321–55.

Gherardi, Evaristo. 1700. *Le Théâtre italien.* 6 vols. Paris: Cusson et Witte.

Gurr, Andrew. 1970. *The Shakespearean Stage: 1574–1642.* Cambridge: Cambridge University Press.

——— 1987. *Playgoing in Shakespeare's London.* Cambridge: Cambridge University Press.

Jomaron, Jacqueline. 1988. *Le Théâtre en France du Moyen Age à 1789.* Paris: Armand Colin.

Lancaster, Henry Carrington. 1940. *The Period of Racine.* Part 4 of *A History of French Dramatic Literature in the Seventeenth Century.* 2 vols. Baltimore: Johns Hopkins Press.

Lough, John. 1959. *Paris Theatre Audiences in the Seventeenth and Eighteenth Centuries.* London: Oxford University Press.

Mélèse, Pierre. 1976. *Le Théâtre et le public à Paris sous Louis XIV.* Geneva: Slatkine.

Molière. 1971. *Oeuvres complètes.* Vol. 1, ed. Georges Couton. Paris: Éditions Gallimard.

Mongrédien, Georges, and Jean Robert. 1981. *Les Comédiens français du XVIIe siècle: Dictionnaire biographique.* Paris: CNRS.

Mousnier, Roland. 1976. *La Stratifications sociale à Paris aux XVIIe et XVIIIe siècles.* Paris: Éditions A. Pedone.

Ravel, Jeffrey S. 1992. "Définir le parterre au XVIIe siècle." In *Ordre et contestation au temps des classiques,* vol. 2, ed. Roger Duchêne and Pierre Ronzeaud. Paris, Seattle, and Tubingen: Papers on French Seventeenth Century Literature, 225–31.

Roy, D. H. 1963. "La Scène de l'Hôtel de Bourgogne." *Revue d'histoire du théâtre* 15:227–35.

Sauval, Henri. 1724. *Histoire et recherches des antiquités de la ville de Paris.* Paris: Moette.

Scott, Virginia. 1990. *The* Commedia dell'Arte *in Paris: 1644–1697.* 3 vols. Charlottesville: University Press of Virginia.

Wiley, W. L. 1960. *The Early Public Theatre in France.* Cambridge: Harvard University Press.

# Symposium Discussion

STANLEY LONGMAN: I would like to ask each symposium panelist to comment on some aspect related to the previous discussions. Then we will open it up for general discussion.

LUIGI ALLEGRI: During the conference, I have not made comments because, quite frankly, I have struggled against a language barrier. Yet, I now recognize with pleasure that I have gained a great deal from these talks. One issue of interest has been the problem of reconstructing historic theatrical spaces. There is no doubt that such endeavors carry both historical and scholarly validity. Nevertheless, they can be dangerous, especially in relation to the public at large. They presuppose that duplicating the architectural context of performance of a period play will enable us to realize its actual text and its genuine cultural world. It is always dangerous to run counter to history, which is what we do when we undertake to duplicate the historical past. It is the sort of thing that we have attempted so often in restoring old churches, for example. We might tear away all the baroque junk to get back to the purely Romanesque church as if no history had passed in the meantime [laughter].

The primary point is not the relationship between the text and the theatrical space; rather, it is the ontological matter of how the play affects the life of the spectator. I may duplicate the physical conditions for which Shakespeare wrote his plays, but I would then have to lay claim to a spectator who does not know television, trains, telephones, or anything that belongs to the modern world. It must be a spectator who shares the same perceptions as Shakespeare. Otherwise, the experiment is doomed, false, and invalid.

Clearly, every script contains within its structure an explicit spatial context for its playing. There is an internal structure for Shakespeare, Pirandello, Calderon, and so forth. It is also clear that every society and culture creates theatrical spaces from its innate, precise sense of space. Every theatre building is a concrete realization of an idea of theatre, and, as such, contains a sense of the play's relationship to the world and to the audience. This fact may strike us as strange inasmuch as the contemporary world entertains many different ideas of reality simultaneously. Yet, until the nineteenth century, the idea of the theatre was substantially that created in the Italian Renaissance. I am not saying this out of chauvinistic nationalism [laughter]. It was an Italian victory, yes, but it was also a hollow victory, a Pyrrhic victory, because we lost an important dimension of the theatrical experience. After all, that victory virtually annihilated all the other options in the way of theatrical structures. The open-air Elizabethan playhouse or the Spanish *corral* are both more interesting for theatrical purposes, more fully adapted to the theatrical experience, which, ultimately, is not really visual. The Italian picture-frame stage has taught us to think of theatre in this visual way, but it is actually a step removed from the true theatrical condition. Instead, the true theatrical condition is the bond created between performer and audience, a bond based on creative collaboration. That bond is by and large absent in the Italianate theatre structure.

LONGMAN: Jay [Allen], would you go next?

JOHN ALLEN: The most appropriate thing to do is to admit part of my own perspective, which might impugn the judgment of those who invited me to come here [laughter]. I started as a professor of Spanish literature who had no interest or connection to the theatre whatsoever, and I remained that way for twenty years. The professional accident of a colleague's retirement got me into the theatre. I began by asking my students to present scenes from the plays they were reading for class. Then, one of them said, "What is the theatre like?" That is what I have been trying to answer for the last fifteen years [laugher].

I had a certain enviable innocence because when I started to study theatre, I did not know anything about these theatres that we have discussed today. Actually, I had only a bunch of repair documents about theatres and the Comba drawing. Perhaps, that innocence allowed me to have the confidence to proceed.

The closest semblance we have to Golden Age theatre are the productions in El Paso [Texas] in the Chamizal Theatre, where they perform Golden Age plays in Spanish once a year to a Spanish-speaking audience that, for the most part, crosses the border. Entire families come to these free performances. The next closest atmosphere of a Golden

Age theatre is in Almargo [Spain], where the townspeople know more about *comedias* than anyone else. They have been going to productions for fifteen years and have become connoisseurs. I am interested more in the audience than the plays because their reactions are as close as we can get to the original. I assume that we read these old plays because they have something to say to us; re-creation of the original atmosphere is an attempt to get closer to the plays, rather than to reconstruct the *corral* theatre or to be at all archeological.

When I started attending plays in Spain, modernization of Lope de Vega consisted of putting a motorcycle on stage. What happens is, you do not trust the text, so you modernize it and take material out. You do not trust the "poor theatre," they call it the "naked stage," and so you dress it up and elaborate on it. The audiences laugh more at the comedies when there are no theoretical conceptions by the director. Similarly, the comic plays are infinitely more successful when they are not elaborately costumed in a nineteenth-century fashion. The audience reactions provide justification for producing Golden Age plays. This renewal has created an excitement among directors who are interested in staging different kinds of productions than they are used to. The entire process is new in the Spanish theatre; before, the presentation of Golden Age plays was so far from the truth. Now, at least we understand something of what they were doing.

The advantage of this conference for me is that it relates immediately to my own concerns—the groundlings, for example. When Andrew Gurr talks about the pricing of things, and the economics of Elizabethan theatre, I realize that we are far from that kind of detailed knowledge in regard to the Spanish stage. So, this is extraordinarily valuable for me as a Hispanist, as a literature person rather than a drama person, to be with people who are involved with acting. I really appreciate the invitation enormously. Thank you.

LONGMAN: Andy [Gurr], would you like to be next?

ANDREW GURR: I am obviously starting with Ron [Vince]'s paper that raised this whole question of reconstruction, and the kind of principle that Luigi raised. I think these concerns are absolutely fundamental. I am not saying that reconstructing a theatre in itself, trying to redesign a theatre, is not of use unless you have a very precise concept of its function. There is a great deal to be gained from precisely reconstructing the machinery of a theatre; however, as the Globe had relatively little machinery, there is not a great deal to be gained from attempting a reconstruction of that kind. There is a lot to be gained from reconstructing it with as accurate materials as possible for the sake of the acoustics and other factors. Yet, there is a major limitation which always involves the audience.

However, there is something distinctive about the Globe that does not quite apply to most of the other theatres. In various ways, it applies quite intriguingly to Molière's theatre, which was not so dissimilar from Shakespeare's in that he was a member of the company, knew his audiences, constructed his metatheatrical jokes in similar kinds of ways. There are distinct resemblances. On the other hand, there are not any theatres we have looked at in which the chief playwright, the person who was writing plays for it, was also owner of 12.5 percent of its equity and was present while it was being designed and built. I mean, that's got some potency! If you add the peculiar difficulties we have with Shakespeare's plays—what remains are just the words he wrote for his actors to memorize. Since he thought of them as plays to be realized on stage, he did not bother to get half of them into print during his lifetime; and if *Henry VIII* had not been shown in July 1613, we would not have the half that he did get into print. That kind of factor makes the Globe significant, I think.

Today, I tend to think of the ways we are familiar with Shakespeare as a bit like reading a film script. Maybe reading Shakespeare is more exciting than some film scripts, but you still do not have the actual, realized entity. I know that reconstructing the audience is in all serious ways impossible, but that does not mean that it is not worth doing. There is a lot to be learned. I have been collecting examples over the last year of aspects to be experimented with in the plays. For instance, whether the remarkably frequent occurrence of a two-line delay between somebody coming in and joining the conversation does not signal the amount of time it took to get from the door in the front scenery out to the front of the stage. Wonderful things strike me, like Malvolio's entry cross-gartered and yellow-stockinged in *Twelfth Night*. In all the editions, you see "Enter Malvolio," and the lady says, "How now, Malvolio?" in great surprise and love. If you go back to the *Folio*, you find it is already entered two lines before, when she is saying she is mad with love, and he has had two lines to register what she is saying, before she sees him. The implications, in terms of the complexity of that entry, are very substantial: the actors have got a lot to learn about eye contact, which all modern Shakespearean actors are taught never to engage in with audiences. We need to experiment with the different features of Shakespeare's plays in the hope, the not entirely unrealistic hope, I think, that we might learn a little more about what the plays were designed to do to their audiences. We do not necessarily need to reconstruct the designed impact in modern conditions—we do not have a realistic hope of doing so. Yet, there seems to be a very substantial process of learning that we could go through.

I would leave myself with the question—I would like to direct it to everybody here—whether that kind of immediacy of association of a particular body of plays with a particular playhouse is quite replicated in the other playhouses we have been talking about. I am not claiming primacy for the Globe, of course, but I wonder whether there is quite that sort of functionality in designing a reconstruction of the Globe in the reconstructions of other theatres.

LONGMAN: Vicki [Scott]?

VIRGINIA SCOTT: Well, that is a wonderful lead. I would say that it would be possible to reconstruct the Palais-Royal without great difficulty. There is a good ground plan and section from 1673; there are also good descriptions. I think you probably could reconstruct it. But what I am interested in is the fact that nobody is the least bit interested in doing so. One of the things I have been thinking about is that in the country I study, unlike Italy, which has surviving monuments from the period; unlike Spain, which has evidently a lot of archeological evidence; unlike England, which has had a passionate interest in reconstructing the Globe for a very long time—nobody in France seems the least bit interested in reconstructing theatres.

LONGMAN: Vive la France.

SCOTT: Vive la France, right [laughter]. One reason may be that the French assume that their national theatre is in a direct line of descent from the seventeenth-century theatre, and, therefore, there is no need to reconstruct because of this continuous tradition. Certainly, one could expect to learn a good deal about reconstructing the performances of Molière in the seventeenth century by performing them on that stage; but, as far as I know, nobody has ever expressed any interest in doing so. So that is one thing I am going to take away and think about.

I am struck by the differences as much as the similarities. When you teach general survey courses in Renaissance theatre to undergraduate students, you are always looking for similarities, trying to pull everything together in some kind of symbiotic whole. But, I have been really struck by differences in this symposium, particularly what Andy Gurr says about some of the management practices in England—this rather unique experience of the sharing actors being involved in ownership of the theatre. What were the differences in the company between the actors that were sharers and housekeepers, and those who were only sharers? I could really ponder that a lot.

There is something absolutely unique in France which no other country had. Although these sharing actors frequently did not own the actual building that they acted in, or the frame of the building, they did frequently own the stage, the boxes, the galleries, the machines, the scenery, and everything inside the theatre. This procedure derives from the French reconstruction of tennis courts. A company rented a tennis court and paid for everything inside. The first sharing company that actually owned a theatre was the company that formed after Molière's death, when the remnants of his company merged with the Marais and then bought the Théâtre Guenegaud in 1673. Considerably after that date, the company paid for the theatre and then built the new Comédie-Française in 1689. So it did happen in France, but it happened much later. Seeing those differences and speculating about the causes of those differences is really interesting. Andy Gurr has said that this ownership of the Globe was an accident—it turned out to be a very happy accident. The same thing was true in France. The ownership of the interior fittings did not come about by design or because anybody thought it was a good idea, but through necessity.

Finally, I have been mulling over this notion of why academics are not interested in the academic theatre of the period [laughter]. This is a very good question [laughter]. And I have to say, in all honesty—you are right, I am not very interested [laughter]. My chief area of interest is audience, and the relationship between the audience and the repertory and the actors; and particularly as that relationship is expressed in commercial ways—who buys what and why. The academic theatre does not include that aspect, so it has never really intrigued me. This period is the beginning of the professional theatre. From 1550, I am fascinated to see how that enterprise came to be and how it grew. The academic theatre, whether the academies of Italy or the Jesuit theatre in France, has always been somewhat peripheral. Professor Vince?

RON VINCE: John Allen called himself an innocent in this congregation and I confessed to him during one of the coffee breaks that, in fact, I am a parasite [laughter]. Nevertheless, what I am interested in is not academic theatre, but academics. That is, us. In sum, what I got out of the past couple of days was the sense of a nice balance between information and comprehension. I was also delighted to have proved once again that good history is being done without a reconstructed Globe, even by those people who plan to reconstruct it [laughter]. I say this a bit in self-defense because I was accused of being a negative jeremiad who was preaching a counsel of despair that we could never learn anything. That is not what I meant at all [laughter]. Undoubtedly, next week I'll start to roll up my pant legs or something [laughter].

It seems that perhaps reconstruction has been overdone during the last couple of days. I have no objection to people building theatres. I think it's far better than building prisons. I would be delighted to attend any reconstructed Globe, whatever it calls itself, be it on the Bankside or wherever it's going to be in North Carolina [laughter]. Still, I remain a bit unrepentant about my hesitation to support the enterprise. Let me put it this way: I have some unease about the ways which the new Globe is being constructed. It is not enough for scholars to think quotation marks around "authenticity" when publicity, newspapers, and brochures are, in fact, doing their best to remove those quotation marks. I understand why the quotation marks are there because I appreciate the deep scholarship that went into that project. After all, John Orrell's book sells in Canada for $61.85, and I purchased it [laughter].

There is the necessity of conniving with this generalized type of tourist-trap notion in order to get the theatre built—to do all those wonderfully good things that scholars want to do. The intentions may in fact be pure; I suspect the intentions have been somehow contaminated by the process. This predilection represents my personal unease with the situation. I sense on occasion, and I hope I'm wrong—of course, everyone will assure me that I am [laughter]—that there seems to be a kind of residual contempt for the public which is supposedly going to be educated by this structure, a contempt that shows itself in the process by which the darned thing got there in the first place. There is a bit of cheating going on: "It is authentic. It is authentic." The quotation marks are not there. The quotation marks are in Professor Gurr's head—and on occasion in his book—but on other occasions they are not there. I realize that I might be offending people, but I do not intend to do that. I just feel uneasy. Perhaps my feeling about reconstruction can be put down this way: Back a million years or so ago when I was twelve years old—you see, all the psychology is coming in [laughter]—I was studying British history, because, as you know, in a former colony [Canada], I was still being subjected to this study [laughter]. My teacher told us about the original, authentic battle-ax that had had seven new handles and three new heads, but it was the "authentic thing" [laughter]. And I've been suspicious of that kind of thing ever since. I'll leave it at that for now.

LONGMAN: I thank all of you very much.

# A Brief Shining Moment

## An Effect That Disappeared from the Illusionistic Stage

### Frank Mohler

"The heavens parted, revealing an assembly of gods with Jupiter in their midst on a golden throne . . . expanding until it filled the entire width of the stage, the celestial machine moved forward on a horizontal plane then descended vertically."

—Marcello Bulligli, description of *Aminta*, 1628

T HE MOST SPECTACULAR effects on the seventeenth-century illusionistic stage were, undoubtedly, those occurring above the stage. Many of the celestial effects that were developed during the seventeenth century became standard on the stages of the eighteenth century. One of the most impressive effects, however, seems to have declined in favor: it was a machine that enabled a device to travel through the sky from upstage to downstage, then expand to fill the stage. The machinery for this effect is not a part of any extant eighteenth-century theatre, nor is it shown in the theatre drawings of the period. Four plates in Diderot's *Encyclopédie* show a machine capable of longitudinal travel, but this machine did not expand, and its operation is not adequately explained.

The demise of the effect may be due to the special requirements for its operation: (1) there must be longitudinal tracks (running upstage-downstage) or some other method of moving the machine from its upstage to its downstage positions; (2) the machine must move through or under the masking borders; (3) the machine itself must provide for the expansion and lowering of the effect; and (4) there must be a method of pulling the machine downstage. Although no single source

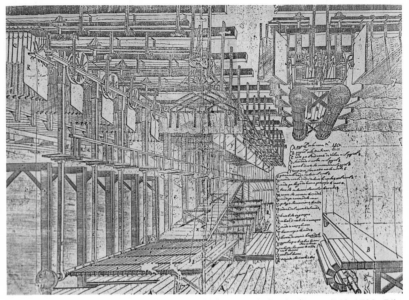

Fig. 7 Seventeenth-Century Machine for Flight toward the Audience (MS 3708, Biblioteca Palatina, Parma)

from the seventeenth-century illustrates or describes all the machinery required for this effect, three sources show machinery that would achieve parts of it.

Manuscript 3708 from the Bibliotèca Palatina is the most complete source, illustrating the tracks, the border passage, and the device used to expand and lower the effect; however, there is no accompanying commentary to describe how the machinery worked. In addition, there are internal inconsistencies within the drawings, and the rigging shown is incomplete. The drawing in the Palatina manuscript (fig. 7) is very detailed and is twice the size of the other drawings in the collection. It is the only source that shows all the tracks necessary for the complete celestial effect. Some of the drawings in this manuscript have been identified as scenes from *La Divisione del Mondo,* an opera presented in Venice in 1675 and designed by Domenico Mauro (Molinari 48–64).[1]

Fabrizio Carini Motta's *Construction of Theatres and Theatrical Machinery,* a 1688 manuscript from the Biblioteca Estense in Modena, Italy, includes some of the necessary tracks and several methods of open-

---

[1]The 1676 San Salvatore manuscript from the Bibliothèque de l'Opéra in Paris also illustrates a method of moving machinery downstage and a technique for lowering and for expanding the effect. This machinery, however, is very different from that shown in the Palatina manuscript.

ing the borders (Larson 95–112). However, Motta does not describe a machine that would use the tracks. This manuscript is the only one that both describes and illustrates the devices.

## Longitudinal Tracks

One of the basic problems related to the effect is that longitudinal tracks must run perpendicular to the main beams of the theatre. These beams run from one side of the theatre to the other to accommodate the machinery for the lateral flying machines and changeable borders. Motta states, "Above all, the most convenient are the tracks that run laterally [longitudinally] from back to front of the stagehouse for the movement of aerial effects toward the audience. . . . they are seldom used because I believe they complicate the hanging of sky borders, ceiling pieces and other items" (Larson 95).

In the Palatina manuscript, there are two types of longitudinal tracks that are used to bring the machine to the front of the theatre: permanent tracks in the upstage or inner stage area, and a combination of permanent and movable hanging brackets in the downstage area. The permanent tracks are hung from the lateral beams of the theatre. In both the upstage and downstage areas, there are three sets of tracks or brackets to allow the passage of a three-part machine.

The upstage tracks are similar in function to the tracks that Motta includes in his *Twelfth Discourse* (Larson 95–112), "The Arrangement of Things Necessary for Aerial Operations" (fig. 8). It is obvious that a track running longitudinally would prevent a lateral border frame from being lowered into view. Motta solves that problem by extending his track only a short distance into the downstage area; there is room for four flying borders downstage of the longitudinal tracks. He shows two sets of longitudinal tracks, one above the other, and discusses the flanking catwalks that would be used to service the machines using the track.

The Palatina manuscript shows a solution to the problem associated with longitudinal tracks in the downstage area. Unique hanging brackets allow the machine to continue to move downstage beyond the permanent tracks to the front of the stage. The sky borders over the downstage area are arranged on travelers to enable them to be pulled to the sides as shown in the upper part of figure 7. At the center of each border a door is hinged to a special bracket that travels with the border. These brackets are suspended from the border traveler tracks, which in turn are attached to the lateral beams of the theatre. As the machine moved downstage and approached each border, the border door would open to allow the machine to pass through to the next bracket.

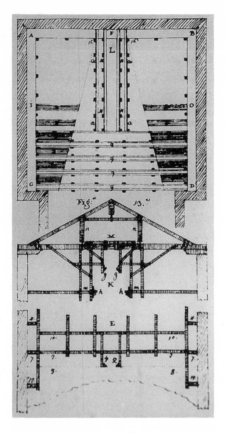

Fig. 8 Tracks for Flight toward the Audience (Motta, *Twelfth Discourse*, Plate 8)

## Border Opening

Motta describes three methods of opening the border to allow a machine to pass downstage. Each of the techniques includes a center section that is composed of cloth flaps supported by whalebone staves. He states, "when the machines . . . move through these borders, the flaps give way then flap back in place" (Larson 105).

The border is split in the middle, and each half can also travel offstage on a lateral track. The partially framed unit is suspended on wheels that serve as traveler carriers and can be pulled on and offstage by rotating a winch.

## Machine

The machine illustrated in the Palatina manuscript consists of three parts: a center unit riding on the permanent center track, and two side

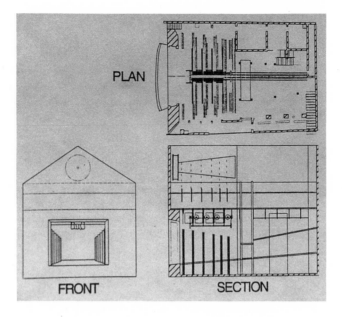

PLAN

FRONT    SECTION

Fig. 9 Flight Reconstruction 2 (Based on MS 3708, Biblioteca Palatina, Parma)

units that rest upon the traveling brackets. The center section consists of a platform controlled by winches mounted on the center track. Each side section consists of a rolling floor with one end attached to the center platform, as shown in the lower right detail in figure 7; the other end wraps around an axle that is suspended by a telescoping unit.

As the borders open, pulling the hanging brackets with the rolling floor units to the side, the floor unrolls as shown in the lower left detail of figure 7. After the unit has been expanded to the side, the entire machine lowers toward the stage floor, controlled both by the winches supporting the center platform and by the telescoping units supporting the axle of the rolling floor. Assuming the machine was masked by clouds, the complete effect would appear as follows.

Prior to the revelation of the effect, the flying borders and the rear shutter or drop, acting together, hide the upstage area. The borders are flown out and the shutter or drop at the rear of the scene is removed, revealing a cloud in the sky at the rear of the inner stage. The cloud travels toward the audience, passing through the borders until it is over the downstage area (fig. 9). The border and the side brackets, now holding the machine, move toward the side of the stage, unrolling a flying stage floor (fig. 10). After the machine has expanded to the sides, performers could step from the catwalks onto the flying stage floor. Finally, all parts of the machine are lowered (fig. 11).

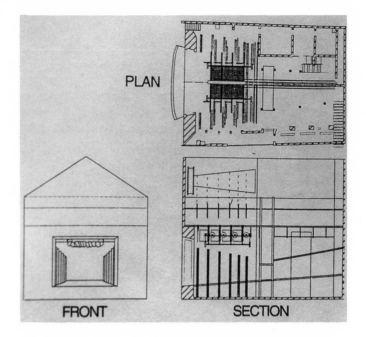

PLAN

FRONT

SECTION

Fig. 10 Flight Reconstruction 3 (Based on MS 3708, Bibliotèca Palatina, Parma)

It would seem that there would be great difficulties, for the large machine has to extend five to six feet beyond one supporting bracket before it comes in contact with the next bracket. In addition, since the brackets are hung from a lateral track, they could be somewhat misaligned as the machine approaches (fig. 9). The distance the machine can be lowered is restricted by the length of the sleeves of the telescoping unit, which, in turn, are limited by the height of the hanging brackets through which they must pass and the border that would mask it.

One missing element for creation of the effect is the method of pulling the three-part machine to the downstage position. Presumably, a cable attached to a winch would be used. A cable between the front of the machine and a winch at the downstage position would interfere with the flying borders and lateral flying machines. However, because the Palatina machine is very long, a cable attached to the back of the machine and running to a winch at the rear of the downstage area would cause less interference.

Perhaps, the difficulties associated with having this celestial effect advance toward the audience were responsible for its disappearance from the illusionistic stage. The only eighteenth-century evidence of this type of machine is in Diderot's *Encyclopédie*. Four plates in the *Ency-*

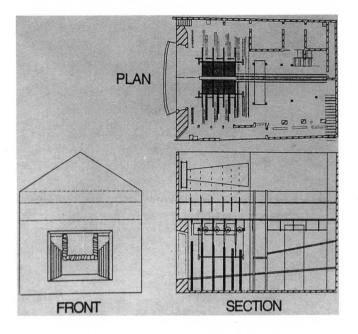

Fig. 11 Flight Reconstruction 4 (Based on MS 3708, Biblioteca Palatina, Parma)

*clopédie* illustrate parts of a machine that flew five units on a diagonal path from the floor in the upstage area to over the downstage area. Although the machine used tracks, similar to the upstage tracks in the Palatina manuscript, the drawings in the *Encyclopédie* do not explain how the machine operated—that is, unless all overhead masking was removed and the machine was rigged immediately prior to its use (Ault 276). Unlike Motta's tracks, which stop at midstage, the *Encyclopédie* shows the tracks continuing downstage, ending near the proscenium. The machinery illustrated in the *Encyclopédie* creates problems rather than solves them.

In spite of the fact that several manuscripts show machinery capable of creating this flight of a large celestial display toward the audience, the difficulty of producing the effect seems to have eliminated it from the smaller court theatres of the eighteenth century. Even the larger Palais-Royal Opera House in Paris included only a reduced version of the machinery. Skipping several centuries, the techniques of the seventeenth century have been brought back to the twentieth-century stage. Computer control and stronger materials have provided new means of creating effects that advance toward the audience for the spectacular musicals currently in vogue on Broadway.

## Works Cited

Ault, Thomas. 1983. "Design, Operation and Organization of Stage Machinery at the Paris Opera: 1770–1873." Ph.D. dissertation, University of Michigan, Ann Arbor.

Larson, Orville. 1987. *The Theatrical Writings of Fabrizio Carini Motta*. Carbondale: Southern Illinois University Press.

MS 3708. Biblioteca Palatina, Parma, Italy.

Molinari, Cesare. 1965. "Disegni a Parma per uno Spettacolo Veneziano." *Critica d'Arte* 47–64, 70.

Nagler, A. M. 1964. *Theatrical Festivals of the Medici: 1539–1637*. New Haven: Yale University Press.

*Recueil de Planches sur les arts Méchaniques avec leur explication*. 1762–72. In *Encyclopédie*, vol. 10, ed. Denis Diderot and Jean le Rond d'Alembert. Paris: Chez Brisson.

Res. C853. Bibliothèque de l'Opéra, Paris.

# Decking the Hall

## Italian Renaissance Extension
## of Performance Motifs
## into Audience Space

### Thomas A. Pallen

"[T]he city can lie within the theatre and the theatre within the hall, as conversely the hall can lie within the theatre and the theatre within the city, etc."[1]

—Ferroni, *"Il teatro e la corte"*

IN HER EXCELLENT treatment of *scenografia* for the *Enciclopedia dello spettacolo,* Elena Povoledo (1964) meticulously traced Italian Renaissance development of that art from the *Città ferrarese* to Vasari's *strada lunga.*[2] Parallel to this series of experiments in spatial use and meaning ran another—one that asked, not what the stage and its scenery should communicate, but what message the *sala* should send, a question alien to modern architectural and scenographic practice.[3]

---

[1] *"La città può essere dentro il teatro e il teatro dentro la sala, come per converso la sala può essere dentro il teatro e il teatro dentro la città, ecc."* (Ferroni 178). This and all Italian sources were translated by the author, with the exception of quotations from Minor and Mitchell's translation of Giambullari.

[2] Povoledo describes the *città ferrarese* (Ferraran city, named for the d'Este court city where it originated) as "a series of houses aligned in a single row, as in the juxtaposed medieval French scene." Without actually using the term *strada lunga,* she describes Vasari's achievement as a "continuous vista, with central axis and a single focus placed beyond the stage wall but not beyond the horizon line." Zorzi (1977, 99) provides the term itself.

[3] Although *sala* literally means "hall," and thus any large indoor space, Margherita Sergardi (115) refers to *sala* as a "generic term that indicates the main hall of a *palazzo* or building, where in the 16th century one constructed the 'stage' (temporary or permanent) to perform for a privileged audience shows, games, or scenic festivals, often of a celebrative nature." In the context of this article, *sala* refers more specifically to the area of a temporary theatre reserved for the audience, which we would call the auditorium.

Modern theatre spectators find themselves in more or less decorated but decisively disengaged auditorium spaces, disengaged, that is, from both the production on stage and the occasion of its performance. For even the most presentational of productions, Diderot's famous wall surgically separates the festive, fictive, engaged stage platform and the scenery, costumes, lighting, and movement, prepared specifically for the spectacle at hand, from its comparatively anonymous counterpoise. Thus, today's theatre critics and commentators remark vividly and sometimes viciously about the production, but almost never about the decor of the house.[4] Not so in Renaissance Italy. As Fabrizio Cruciani has noted, "the oft-time asserted hall-stage union is not a matter of the presence and utilization of elements of separation or communication, but of the unified conception of the apparatus, which is both of the stage and of the hall, often enough with a continuum that may be formal, that is always thematic" (37–38). When Giorgio Vasari recorded the theatrical works of Italian artists in his *Vite de' più eccellenti Pittori, Scultori et Architettori* (*Lives of the Most Excellent Painters, Sculptors and Architects*),[5] he frequently established an equilibrium between the two spaces. Four such instances of decorated auditoriums stand out due to their thematic natures.

The first decorated hall noted by Vasari comes from the year 1513 in the city of Urbino. For a production of *La Calandria*, Girolamo Genga amended the *Città ferrarese* by extending it into the *sala* (Vasari 1912–14, 7:200). Baldassare Castiglione, in a letter to Lodovico Canossa, described the effect: "the foot of the stage very naturally showed a reproduction of the city wall with two towers, one at each end of the room: in one stood the pipers, in the other the trumpet players. In the middle was another well-formed flank: the auditorium remained like the city moat, traversed by two walls as if to restrain the water."[6] Scholars have disagreed as to the exact placement of that second, outer "moat" wall. Povoledo, for example, suggested that it may have been a "bulwark for the lowest tier of seating" (1975, 379) (fig. 12). Perhaps with this location in mind, Giovanni Attolini has con-

---

[4]Productions such as those created for Webber's *Starlight Express* or Bernstein's *Candide*, which seemingly reunite audience and stage space, in fact further emphasize the distance between them. The result is not a fulfillment of Richard Schechner's third axiom but a fracturing of the audience-performer disengagement into multiple copies of itself.

[5]Translated by Gaston Du C. DeVere (London: Philip Lee Warner, 1912–14).

[6]The complete text of Castiglione's letter has appeared in numerous sources, among them Ruffini (197–99). Another account of the same occasion, *Ms. Vat. Ubr. Lat. 490* (*cc. 193v–196v*), also reprinted by Ruffini (200–203), makes no mention of the moat effect.

cluded that the "moat" may have remained empty (114). At the other extreme, the moat wall could have stood at the far end of the hall from the stage, a possibility noted and negated by Povoledo (1975, 398 n. 15). Cesare Molinari, on the other hand, theorized that the duke and his immediate court viewed the performance from within Genga's moat, while the remainder of the spectators found places on grandstands placed along the walls beyond it (147). The typical audience arrangement of Italian court theatres distinguished between a princely party grouped on and around a rostrum placed in the hall's midst along the visual axis of the scenery on stage, and the remainder of the audience seated on a U-shaped grandstand (fig. 13). Although the arrangement suggested by Povoledo and depicted in Figure 12 involves a stageward displacement of the rostrum, it seems a likely choice, for it would call even more attention to the duke.[7]

Whether the ducal party sat within the moat or beyond it, the fact

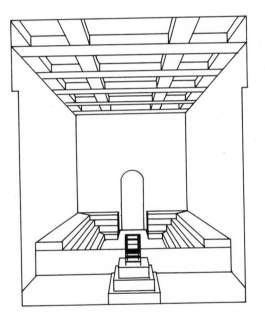

Fig. 12 Genga's Hall According to Povoledo and Molinari (Thomas A. Pallen)

---

[7]Attolini notes that "The only spectators involved in the performance were in reality the lords, the princes; involved to the point of offering themselves as spectacle. So much so that they were customarily seated on a platform at the center of the hall, completely separated from the rest of the audience" (114).

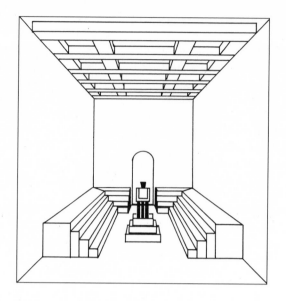

Fig. 13 Typical Italian Seating Arrangement (Thomas A. Pallen)

remains that Genga had not only modified the *Città ferrarese* but had extended its physical identity and presence into the *sala*.[8]

Having noted the parallel between the two-towered city of Genga's scene and Urbino's own twin-towered palace, and also the symbolic relationship among city, palace, and throne room, Franco Ruffini stated,

> It was not so much a matter of enclosing the spectators in the scenery . . . as of rounding off, even formally, the image of the city. If we like, this is only the extreme extent of the figurative tautology: the datum for an instinctive reading of the *entire hall as scene* and thus as city.
>
> The scene extends into the hall because the scene *is* the hall and, vice-versa, because the hall *is* the scene. (168–69)

The hall is the scene, or, to translate the Italian another way, the hall is the stage—at least for Genga at Urbino. Seated on his rostrum within the moat, the duke became not only figuratively but physically identified with the idealized city depicted on the stage.

Other scenographers would endow their halls with other meanings.

---

[8]Ruffini discusses the placement of the second wall thoroughly, ending by accepting Povoledo's theory because it "reproduces, adapted to the *sala*, the guiding ideal of the ancient theatre, balanced toward a *cavea* enclosing the auditorium seats" (147 ff.). In other words, the space within Genga's moat paralleled the Roman orchestra, where honored spectators sat, while the U-shaped grandstand resembled the surrounding *cavea*.

Twenty-six years later, for example, in Florence, Bastiano da San Gallo erected a theatre in the second courtyard of the Medici palace in via Larga (now known as Palazzo Medici-Riccardi). The 1539 marriage of Cosimo de' Medici and Eleonora of Toledo provided the occasion. San Gallo, called Aristotile, suspended a cloth sky over the courtyard that served "to protect the guests from the evening chill and dampness and to augment the illusion, helping to give the courtyard the appearance of an enclosed hall" (Mamone 34). From this artificial sky, or ceiling, San Gallo "suspended a good number of lascivious little cupids with bows and arrows and a lighted torch in the hands of each; with these they illuminated the place and frolicked in various attitudes above the handsome and honored company" (Giambullari).[9]

On the courtyard walls to each side of the stage, twelve paintings, meticulously described by Vasari, depicted great deeds from the bride-groom's life (Vasari 1912–14, 8:13). Grouped in two series of six paint-ings each, they ranged in subject from Cosimo's return from exile to the marriage of Francesco de' Medici and Margherita d'Austria in Naples. This laudatory and biographical time machine served both to extol Cosimo and to complement the production's intermezzi. Attolini provides the following description of those interludes, written by Giovanbattista Strozzi, with music by Francesco Corteccia:[10]

> The first intermezzo, whose action took place during the morning, brought on stage twelve shepherd couples variously costumed; the sec-ond, which took place at midday, introduced three nude Sirens with tails meticulously decorated with silver scales, three Nymphs covered by a pale green veil, and three marine Monsters with rams' horns; the third, imag-ined as taking place in the afternoon, had Silenus as its protagonist; the fall of evening coincided with the fourth and included stage action by some nymphs. The complete number of intermezzi was six, including the prologue and epilogue. As is evident, the passage of time furnished the narrative thread: the show opened with Aurora rising in the heavens of the stage and closed with Night who, lowered from the ceiling, an-nounced in song the final dance of the Satyrs and Bacchantes. (145)

Nino Pirrotta, who provides a far more detailed account of Corteccia's intermezzi, notes that they in fact carried forth two themes—honor to the royal couple and progression of time: "The intervals thus paid due

---

[9]Among others, Mamone comments at length on the Florentine custom of covering not only courtyards but also streets and large piazzas with strips of cloth, adding that in this case Aristotile also had in mind the velarium used to cover Roman theatres and amphitheatres, noting as evidence his studies of Vitruvius and similar echoes of Roman practices (34–35).

[10]For biographical notes on all the artists involved in this production, see Minor and Mitchell, 24–31 and 56–58.

homage to the ducal couple. . . . But their principal theme is the continuity of time and their function was that of creating the illusion of that continuity, constrained by temporal perspective within the shorter time of the performance" (174).

As already suggested, these intermezzi functioned in accord with Aristotile's *sala*—the twelve paintings reminding everyone of the past while Cosimo himself represented the present. Moreover, both the intermezzi and *sala* decor harmonized with the play and its scenography, a most unusual occurrence for an Italian Renaissance *festa*. The plot of Landi's comedy depends heavily on the passage of time and its characters frequently comment on this subject (Pirrotta 175). Although Pirrotta has observed that the "Characters and themes of every intermezzo are new and have no rapport either among themselves or with the main plot (except that of being the hands of a clock)," her parenthetical phrase precisely identifies the point of juncture between intermezzi and main plot. Aristotile's staging featured a prominent scenographic device carefully calculated to further spin out this predominant temporal thread. As the performance unfolded, an illuminated, artificial sun slowly moved through the sky, marking the progress of the day (Vasari 1912–14, 8:9).[11]

Scenography, script, *sala*, and intermezzi shared the theme of Time. However, while the play, its intermezzi, and Aristotile's sun emphasized tight continuity, the *sala* paintings accomplished the opposite. The chronology conveniently omitted all events that would depict the Medici in a poor light or address their absence from Florentine rule. As Minor and Mitchell point out, the paintings and other courtyard decorations had the goal of positioning Cosimo clearly as the successor to earlier Medici rulers (18). San Gallo's decor also echoed, if somewhat ironically, the motto set by Lorenzo il Magnifico for his family, his city, and the Italian Renaissance in general: *le tems revient* ("time renews itself" or "the [great] times return").[12]

Time occupied Vasari himself in 1542, when a Venetian *compagnia della calza*, the Sempiterni, hired him to design scenery and a temporary

---

[11]Interpretative models built by Ferdinando Ghelli of this setting and its artificial sun appeared in a show dedicated to scenographic devices titled, *Il cavallo di Troia. Macchine e meccanismi scenici e letterari* (*The Trojan horse: scenic and literary machines and devices*), held at Montefalco in 1993. The model of the overall setting has three-dimensional steps leading from ground level to stage level, rather than the illusionistically painted stairway described by Vasari, and includes a *cielo a bote* (barrel-shaped sky), of which Vasari makes no mention (*Il cavallo* 76–77).

[12]The "time" referred to in the Medici motto was the proverbial "golden age" cited in its source, Virgil's fourth eclogue. See Ventrone (1992).

theatre for their production of Pietro Aretino's *La Talanta*. In a letter to Ottaviano de' Medici describing this production, Vasari paid greatest attention to the hall decor he had devised, a scheme that mingled time and geography.

He devoted the ceiling to Time, filling it with painted panels that allegorically portrayed the four stages of the day, each surrounded by smaller panels containing anthropomorphic depictions of the hours pertinent to it. At the center of the composition appeared Chronos himself, dispersing the hours through space (Vasari 1906, 8:284). Attention to Time seems appropriate to the production's patrons, the Sempiterni, whose name means "eternal" or "everlasting." Their Venetian location, in turn, inspired the eight geographic wall paintings, four per side, containing figurative representations of the major rivers of the Veneto.

Attolini feels that with this decor, Vasari "achieved the notion of prolonging the historical-artistic allegory of the scenography from the center of the stage to the decoration of the auditorium" (124). Although it is difficult to comprehend how allegorical paintings of the Veneto extended the scenography, which depicted the city of Rome, into the auditorium, Vasari's ceiling paintings certainly made an excellent accompaniment to his stage lighting furnished by "a sun which, moving during the performance, provided a very strong light" (Vasari 1906, 8:284). Vasari thus took Aristotile's lighting device and extended its symbolism to the auditorium by means of paintings that depicted not only the compass points of the sun's daily journey but also each individual hour of the twenty-four that humanist interpreters of the *Poetics* condoned in dramatic poets' plots.

Vasari's *sala* decorations for a production of Francesco D'Ambra's *La Cofanaria* in 1565 concentrated on geography alone. This performance, a relatively small part of the three-month *festa* held to celebrate and solemnize the marriage between Francesco de' Medici and Joan of Austria, took place in the large hall called the Salone dei Cinquecento, in Palazzo Vecchio.[13] Vasari designed the play's scenery, which consisted of a wing-and-shutter depiction of the Piazza Santa Trinita and via di Maggio area of Florence. He also completely remodeled the Salone, whose new decor included ten large wall paintings depicting the major squares of cities subject to Florence. The placement of these paintings, as well as that of smaller ceiling panels, followed a precise geographical schema that placed Tuscan cities at wall and ceiling positions that corresponded to their directions from Florence (Starn and Partridge 176).

---

[13]For full accounts of this production and the *festa* in general, see Vasari (1912–14, 9:105; 1906, 8:572).

On this occasion, Vasari effectively placed Duke Francesco in the midst of his realm, with two-dimensional framed views to two sides of and above him and a three-dimensional realization of Florence on the stage. Whereas Genga had extended the scene into the hall, where it encompassed the duke of Urbino, Vasari melded hall and stage together, surrounding the ruler of Florence with his realm.

Vasari, who clearly expected thematic engagement between *sala* and stage, would probably find today's disengaged theatres uncomfortably odd. Yet there are explanations we could offer for the change, the most obvious being the disengagement between theatre design and scenography, between architect and scenographer. Genga, Aristotile, and Vasari created temporary theatres intended to house a single production and could therefore link the entire space to a single image or theme, which they called the *invenzione*. Andrea Palladio, whom Vasari mentions only briefly in the *Lives,* was among the first to cleave theatre design from scenic design. In part, this split occurred because Palladio's death left Vincenzo Scamozzi to add the now famous scenic vistas to the Teatro Olimpico schema,[14] but in a sense it originated when Palladio accepted the Olympic Academy's commission to design and build a permanent theatre intended to house multiple productions. Such a commission, completely unlike those accepted by Genga, Aristotile, and Vasari, obliterated thematic connections between stage and *sala*.

Another point of disengagement between these two spaces, which we, in the footsteps of Diderot, think of as separate artistic entities, lies in the fulfillment of the French encyclopedist's vision of the imaginary wall between them. Genga, Aristotile, and Vasari designed their engaged-space theatres at least partly as a reflection of the active engagement caused by the fact that performers freely crossed between stage and *sala*. As Mamone notes in regard *to Il commodo:*

> Access to the raised stage came from the hall, since a solution that rendered the stage self-sufficient had not yet been arrived at and since the actors were not traveling professionals but amateurs who had full rights in the society of the spectators; they could thus remain in front of the stage until the moment when the play required them on stage. While waiting to play their part, or in the lengthy intervals between one appearance and the next, they remained seated in the first rows (36–37).

We, on the other hand, prefer for the most part to keep our actors out of the audience. In the absence of a homogeneity of traffic, of the social identity between actors and audience cited by Mamone, homoge-

---

[14]Whether Scamozzi simply realized designs already devised by Palladio or truly invented the Olimpico's scenic vistas is a moot point as regards the current discussion. For a thorough examination of the question, however, see Magagnato (47 ff.).

neity of decor no longer seems appropriate or necessary. The further absence of homogeneity of design, brought about by the disengagement of architect from scenographer, makes homogeneity of decor nearly impossible.

Finally, there is the effect of light. In every instance where Vasari finds himself stimulated to describe the lighting effects created for provisional theatres, he pays equal attention, as did the scenographers whose work he records, to the illumination of the stage and the *sala*. It is clear that they saw light as another element of thematic unity, of engagement between these spaces. We, on the other hand, deliberately use light to disengage them.

In recent decades, numerous theatre experimenters have attempted to de-emphasize the distinction between performers and audience members, between stage and auditorium. Yet, the productions described here presented a greater degree of engagement, of total environment, than their modern descendants. The difference, as the examples of Genga, Aristotile, and Vasari demonstrate, lies not so much in the nature of the effort as in patronage and economics. Whereas a vast and diverse public supports today's theatre, with each "patron" paying a very small percentage of the cost, a single patron paid the entire cost of the sixteenth-century Italian productions cited here. For the scenographers who served those single patrons, engagement between hall and stage was an easily accomplished necessity rather than a financially out-of-reach production concept. Vasari and his coevals possessed not only the desire but the means to deck the halls.

## Works Cited

Attolini, Giovanni. 1988. *Teatro e spettacolo nel Rinascimento*. Rome and Bari: La Terza.

Cruciani, Fabrizio. 1987. "Il teatro e la festa." In *Il teatro italiano nel Rinascimento,* ed. Fabrizio Cruciani and Daniele Seragnoli. Bologna: Il Mulino.

Ferroni, Giulio. 1987. "*Il teatro e la corte.*" In *Il teatro italiano nel Rinascimento,* ed. Fabrizio Cruciani and Daniele Seragnoli. Bologna: Il Mulino.

*Il cavallo di Troia. Macchine e meccanismi scenici e letterari*. 1993. Catalog of the exhibition. Reggio Emilia: Tecnostampa.

Magagnato, Licisco. 1992. *Il teatro Olimpico*. Ed. Lionello Puppi. Milan: Electa.

Mamone, Sara. 1981. *Il teatro nella Firenze medicea*. Milan: Mursia.

Minor, Andrew C., and Bonner Mitchell. 1968. *A Renaissance Entertainment: Festivities for the Marriage of Cosimo I, Duke of Florence, in 1539*. Columbia: University of Missouri Press.

Molinari, Cesare. 1974. "Gli spettatori e lo spazio scenico nel teatro del Cinquecento." *Bollettino del Centro internazionale di Studi Andrea Palladio* 16.

Pirrotta, Nino. 1975. *Li due Orfei*. Turin: Einaudi.

Povoledo, Elena. 1964. "Scenografia." In *Enciclopedia dello spettacolo*. Venice and Rome: Istituto per la collaborazione culturale.

———. 1975. "Origini e aspetti della scenografia in Italia. Dalla fine del Quattrocento agli intermezzi fiorentini del 1589." In Nino Pirrotta, *Li due Orfei*. Turin: Einaudi.

Ruffini, Franco. 1983. *Teatri prima del teatro: Visioni dell'edificio e della scena tra Umanesimo e Rinascimento*. Roma: Bulzoni.

Sergardi, Margherita. 1979. *Lingua Scenica: terminologia teatrale nel Cinque-cento* [Stage language: theatrical terminology in the sixteenth century]. 2d revised ed. Firenze: S. T. I. A. V.

Starn, Randolph, and Loren Partridge. 1992. *Arts of Power: Three Halls of State in Italy, 1300–1600*. Berkeley: University of California Press.

Vasari, Giorgio. 1906. "Lettere." In *Le Opere di Giorgio Vasari*, ed. Gaëtano Milanesi. 9 vols. Florence, 1878–85. Paperback edition. Florence: Sansoni.

———. 1912–14. *Lives of the Most Eminent Painters, Sculptors and Architects*. 10 vols. Trans. Gaston DuC. DeVere. London: Philip Lee Warner.

Ventrone, Paola. 1992. "Feste e spettacoli nella Firenze di Lorenzo il Magnifico." In *Le Tems revient / 'l Tempo si rinuova*. Ed. Paola Ventrone. Florence: Silvana.

Zorzi, Ludovico. *Il teatro e la città: saggi sulla scena italiana*. Milan: Einaudi, 1977.

# Oppositional Staging in Shakespeare's Theatre

## Franklin J. Hildy

W HEN THE FOUNDATIONS of the Elizabethan Rose play-house were excavated in London from December 1988 to June 1989, its wide, shallow, tapered stage was one of its most prominent features.[1] The width of the stage at its broadest point—thirty-six feet, nine inches—was somewhat smaller than scholars might have expected, given the known widths of English Renaissance stages: forty feet for London's first theatre, the Red Lion, and forty-three feet for the Rose's replacement theatre, the Fortune. But then the entire theatre, measuring only seventy-two feet across its polygonal ground plan, was smaller than scholars had anticipated. The depth of the stage, on the other hand, was a real surprise. Estimated at just sixteen feet, five inches for the original Rose stage of 1587, and just eighteen feet, four inches for the renovated stage of 1592, it was substantially shallower than even the small size of the theatre would have led most scholars to expect. The Fortune contract, that Rosetta stone of Elizabethan theatre architecture, had long been interpreted as indicating a stage depth of twenty-seven feet, six inches, and modern scholars had come to believe in it as the standard from which it was unwise to deviate.[2] The archaeological evidence of the Rose offered the first physical evidence calling that standard into question.

Fortunately for my own credibility, I had argued just one month be-

---

[1] Stage dimensions are from Bowsher and Blatherwick (63, 70). After five years this remains the only official published report on the excavation.

[2] The Fortune contract called for a stage extending to the middle of its fifty-five-foot square yard; the Rose stage falls six feet short of the center line of its smaller, polygonal yard.

fore the Rose discovery was announced (in a paper for the Shakespeare Association of America) that Elizabethan stages were unlikely to have been more than eighteen feet in depth (Hildy 1989). I based that argument on an analysis of Renaissance theatre buildings throughout Europe, especially those of Spain.[3] I had come to the simple conclusion that when a large part of an audience stands around a stage that is elevated five feet or more, the actors cannot use more than eighteen feet of stage depth.[4] Indeed, European stages of the period are rarely as deep as that, unless they have been designed to include perspective scenery, and then the stage depth actually used by the actors remains quite shallow. But the Teatro Olimpico at Vicenza, though admittedly not a great success as a theatre, has been a troubling case in point for my argument. Its stage is shallow (the acting platform in front of the facade is only twenty-one feet, four inches deep), but no audience stands around this stage; all audience members occupy seats that look down on it (Kohler 284). A stage of any depth was possible, so why was it limited to just over one quarter of its eighty-two-foot width? Partly, of course, the answer is that the Olimpico was a reconstruction of the theatres of ancient Rome, whose stages, while often one hundred feet or more wide, were rarely over twenty feet deep. But this just moves the question back to the model. Why were Roman stages shallow? What is going on here? One of the things going on, I now believe, was a Renaissance fascination with oppositional staging, and it is the special application of this oppositional staging in theatres of Shakespeare's day that I wish to explore in this essay.

Oppositional staging, by which I mean the tendency for opposing parties to enter at opposite ends of a wide but shallow stage and face off with one another, is an obvious yet effective way to illustrate the conflicts inherent in most dramas. The plays of Shakespeare and his contemporaries are filled with such straightforward visual images as opposing groups of individuals, families, armies, and so forth, meeting on opposite sides of "this unworthy scaffold." The armies in *Julius Caesar*, the families in *Romeo and Juliet*, Hamlet and Laertes crossing swords,

---

[3] I have developed the comparison with Spanish theatres more fully in " 'Think when we talk of horses' " (Hildy 1991).

[4] Even at the height of the baroque picture-frame stages, actors rarely used more than twelve feet of the depth of the stage. A modern analysis of the use of stage space carried out by Jo Mielziner in preparation for the design of the Vivian Beaumont Theatre at Lincoln Center revealed that even in the early 1960s, the dominant action of most Broadway productions took place within ten feet of the curtain line. I want to thank William Condee for calling my attention to this study, which is documented in the Jo Mielziner file at the Performing Arts Library, New York Public Library, Lincoln Center.

the quintessential oppositional staging of Middleton's *A Game at Chess*, are some of the more blatant examples of this tendency.[5] Walter Hodges had a sense of this when he wrote:

> Elizabethan plays lay consistent emphasis at all periods upon movement across the width of the stage—enter on one side, A; and on the other, B, etc. Groups of characters will play on opposite sides of the stage on the common understanding that they are far enough apart to be unaware of each other's presence. . . . On the other hand there is nowhere in any of these plays any particular requirement for action in great depth. . . . In practice nearly all Elizabethan plays would actually be difficult to produce, to any great effect, on a stage featuring depth at the expense of width. (1947, 110)

There is a real irony in this statement. When Hodges wrote it in 1947, tapered stages—like the one discovered at the Rose dig forty-two years later—were assumed to be the norm for Elizabethan playhouses, and numerous theoretical reconstructions of the Globe had included the tapered stage.[6] But Hodges himself soon replaced that standard when he brought forward the arguments based on the rectangular stage shown in the famous deWitt drawing of the singularly unsuccessful Swan playhouse (Hodges 1950, 83–94). Hodges's rectangle led to theoretical approaches like those of J. L. Styan, who argued that Elizabethan plays were unique in their emphasis on "staging in depth," a concept in direct conflict with the tendency for side to side movement that Hodges had observed previously.[7] The tapered stages Hodges had successfully swept from consideration, however, may have served, better than he could possibly have realized, the kind of oppositional staging he intuitively sensed in the plays.

To understand my assertion here we need to return to the issue of stage depth; even the tapered stages of the pre-Hodges era were unworkably deep, which is why their potential for oppositional staging was not more clearly realized. For many years the idea that Elizabethan stages were deep stages rested entirely on the contract for the building of the Fortune theatre. This document was first published by Malone in 1790, but neither he nor his successor, George Chalmers, who expanded Malone's work in 1797, made any attempt to interpret it. It

---

[5]A full analysis of the oppositional staging in *A Game at Chess* can be found in Hotson (1960).

[6]For the most complete visual record of the pre-1950 reconstructions of the Globe, see Stinson.

[7]Styan first discussed this idea in "The Actor at the Foot of Shakespeare's Platform" (1959) but developed it more fully in *Shakespeare's Stagecraft* (1967).

was not until 1831 that J. Payne Collier attempted to explain the document. In his work, *History of English Dramatic Poetry to the Time of Shakespeare and the Annals of the English Stage to the Restoration,* Collier noted that the contract called for "the frame of the saide howse to be sett square" and to measure eighty feet on a side "withoutt" and fifty-five feet on a side "within." The contract then goes on to instruct the contractor, who had just finished building the Globe for Shakespeare and company, to build this theatre "With a Stadge and Tyreinge-howse, to be made erected & sett upp within the saide fframe; with a shadowe or cover over the saide Stadge; which Stage shall be placed & sett, as alsoe stearcases of the said fframe, in suche sorte as is prefigured in a plott thereof drawen: and which Stadge shall conteine in length Fortie and Three foote of lawfull assize, and in breadth to extende to the middle of the yarde of the said howse." Collier interpreted this to mean: "The stage was to project to the middle of the yard, or twenty-seven feet and a half, which, added to the twelve feet interval, before noticed, between the outer and inner frames, would make a depth for the stage and 'tiring-house' (supposing it to be at the back of the stage) of thirty-nine feet and a half" (305).

First of all, the "interval, before noticed" was twelve feet, six inches on the previous page of his book and should have been so here. Collier may have been attempting to silently adjust for the thickness of the outer wall, although six inches scarcely seems thick enough for an external supporting wall. But the essential point is that Collier has assumed that the phrase "within the saide fframe" meant within the external walls of the galleries. Yet, the contract refers to the entire gallery structure as "the frame of saide howse," which would suggest that the instruction for "a Stadge and *Tyreinge-howse,* to be made erected & sett upp within the saide fframe" (italics mine) meant that both structures were to be within one half of the fifty-five-foot yard. A tiring-house with a depth of ten to twelve feet would reduce the depth of the stage from Collier's assumed twenty-seven feet, six inches to seventeen feet, six inches, or even fifteen feet, six inches. The same logic can be applied to the lawsuit documents discovered in 1983 that refer to the Red Lion platform as being forty feet wide by thirty feet deep. If a tiring-house covers ten to twelve feet of that platform, the depth of the stage becomes twenty feet or less. So the evidence for deep stages in the Elizabethan playhouses depends on the interpretation of the documents, while alternative interpretations agree more closely with the most substantial evidence—the archaeology of the Rose site.

Collier did not speculate on the shape of the stage implied by the Fortune contract, but it has always been reproduced as rectangular in spite of the contract's instructions for it to be built "in suche sorte as is prefigured in a plott thereof drawen." That plot was apparently based on the Globe stage, because this section concludes with the instruction to build the stage "in all other propocions contryved and fashioned like unto the Stage of the saide Plaie howse called the Globe," which the contractor had just finished erecting. If the stage was to be a simple rectangle, this admonition to follow the plot hardly seems necessary. But if the stage was to be tapered, like the one at the Rose, the single dimension of forty-three feet hardly seems sufficient. With the drawing attached, however, a single base line is all that is needed. If forty-three feet was the width of the front of the stage, for example, the drawing would let the contractor know exactly how it should widen toward the rear. If forty-three feet was the measure at the back of the stage, the drawing would make it clear exactly how the stage should narrow toward the front. If the stage were to taper toward the front and back, as it does at the Rose, the forty-three feet would indicate the widest point and the drawing would make it clear how to proceed from there. This is not to argue that the Fortune stage must have been tapered; but it does illustrate that the assumption that the stage was rectangular is exactly that: an assumption. My interest here is in the possible value of the tapered stage of the Rose playhouse, which, we must remember, remained tapered even after the renovation of 1592.

The stage of the Rose has been described by the archaeologists who excavated it as an elongated hexagon because it tapers not only toward the front but also toward the rear. I have found it more helpful to think of this stage as being composed of two trapezoids joined along their longest side.[8] But regardless of the description, this double taper was also a feature of the pre-Hodges reconstructions of the Globe. The front taper had been inspired by the well-known illustrations from the frontispieces of the plays *Roxana,* published in 1632, and *Messallina,* published in 1640. No rear taper appears in these vignettes, however. That feature owes its creation, interestingly enough, to the 1907 Archer-Godfrey reconstruction of the Fortune playhouse. In that reconstruction the front of the stage is not tapered but the rear is, in order to allow the two entrance doors of the tiring-house to be placed at oblique angles. The obliquely placed doors were needed, as Archer says, in order to provide "a point on the Upper Stage (that is, the gallery at the back of the stage) from which incidents passing on the Rear Stage should be visible" (165). There has never been adequate evidence for the existence of a rear stage in the Elizabethan playhouses—though some form of reveal space surely existed—so Archer's explanation is a

---

[8]See my analysis of the focal points created on such a stage in Hildy (1994).

rather dubious justification for the existence of a rear taper to these stages. And John Astington has recently argued rather persuasively that the *Roxana* and *Messallina* vignettes were based on a French drawing with no relevance to the theatres of Shakespeare's London, making them suspect evidence for a taper toward the front. Yet, in spite of the suspect nature of the evidence employed, those using it managed to arrive at a stage similar in all respects, except for depth, to the stage discovered at the Rose excavations.

The discovery of the foundations of the Rose playhouse has enabled us to return to the analysis of a type of stage that was theorized seventy-five years ago but has long since been abandoned. In the intervening years, the *Records of Early English Drama* series has taught us a great deal about theatre outside London. This new interest has resulted in the publication of a number of books on the subject—including Alan Nelson's most recent work, *Early Cambridge Theatres,* which describes the stages of the academic theatres used in Cambridge from 1546 until the outbreak of civil war in the next century. The most striking characteristic of these stages is that they are wide, shallow, and have a tiring-house at each end. This same arrangement turns up in many Renaissance re-creations of Roman theatres. It probably reflects a Renaissance interpretation of Vitruvius that suggested that in the theatres of ancient Rome, a door at one end of the stage was accepted as leading to the city, while the door at the other end was seen as leading to the port. This established a clear opposition between natives and visitors. Opposing tiring-houses were one way of suggesting the same dynamic.

To be sure, Leslie Hotson had already noted the existence of this arrangement in the academic theatres as early as the 1950s. He had also noted that it was a characteristic of the professional theatres of sixteenth- and seventeenth-century Spain to use opposing tiring-houses on each end of the stages. Unfortunately, in his 1960 book, *Shakespeare's Wooden O,* Hotson pursued this oppositional dynamic to such extremes that it has been discredited ever since. Unable to conceive of anything other than a very deep rectangular stage for the Elizabethan playhouses, he proposed an impossibly complex scheme that had as many as three tiring-houses on each side of the stage. These tiring-houses were two-storied structures with curtain walls. When not involved in the action of the play, all eight curtains on each unit had to be pulled back to allow the audience to see through the structure, which otherwise blocked the view from both sides. When in use, all the curtains had to be closed. Actors had to enter the structures by way of ladders stuck up through stage traps. Such an arrangement would have involved vast numbers of stagehands and would have made even the greatest dramas of the day merely plays about opening and closing curtains.

If Hotson had access to the Rose archaeology he might have seen a solution to this impossible muddle. The genius of the Rose stage is that it took the opposing tiring-houses of the academic theatres and shifted them into the corners facing the center of the theatre. Now, rather than actors entering from entrances facing one another and meeting in the middle, they entered from doors facing the center point of the stage's front edge. Actors entering from these doors were on a collision course; the audience could see that from the first entrance and anticipated the collision that clearly was going to occur right in their midst.

I described the Rose stage earlier as being composed of two trapezoids joined along their longest sides. The focal point of a trapezoid tends to be at the center of the side opposite the longest one because the angle of the other two sides leads the eye in that direction. For the front trapezoid of the Rose stage, the focal point is exactly where the collision will occur. The focal point for the rear trapezoid is at the back, between the doors. This gives focus to those characters who may be observing the impending collision, or to those characters who make a final comment before retreating from the stage.

Oppositional staging was one of the fundamental dynamics of the reemerging playhouses of the Renaissance. The Rose playhouse represents a unique form of this dynamic, and we have not yet begun to examine its implications for the staging of the drama of the period. How might it have affected the entrances and exits, not to mention the patterns of movements, throughout a complex and subtle play like *Hamlet*? How would such patterns differ from those that will be created by a three-door tiring-house facing straight out onto a rectangular stage, like the one being used by the International Shakespeare Globe Centre for its reconstruction of Shakespeare's Globe in London? Such questions remain to be studied, offering continuing evidence that even in this well-worked field of theatre history, there is still a great deal to be explored.

## List of Works Cited

Archer, William. 1907. "The Fortune Theatre, 1600." *Jahrbuch der Deutschen Shakespeare-Gesellecheft* 44:159–66.

Astington, John. 1991. "The Origins of the *Roxana* and *Messallina* Illustrations." *Shakespeare Survey* 43:149–69.

Bowsher, Julian M. C., and Simon Blatherwick. 1990. "The Structure of the Rose." In *New Issues in the Reconstruction of Shakespeare's Theatre*, ed. Franklin J. Hildy, 55–78. New York: Peter Lang.

Chalmers, George. 1797. "Of the History of the Stage." In *An Apology for the Believers in the Shakespeare Papers, Which Were Exhibited in Norfolk-Street*, 339–471. London: Thomas Egerton.

Collier, J. Payne. 1831. "An Account of the Old Theatres of London." In *The History of English Dramatic Poetry to the Time of Shakespeare: and Annals of the Stage to the Restoration*, vol. 3, 261–450. London: John Murray.

Hildy, Franklin J. 1989. "The Shallow Stage." Paper read at the Shakespeare Association of America convention, Austin, Texas, April.

———, ed. 1990. *New Issues in the Reconstruction of Shakespeare's Theatre*. New York: Peter Lang.

———. 1991. " 'Think when we talk of horses, that you see them'; Comparative Techniques of Production in the Elizabethan and Spanish Golden Age Playhouses." *Text and Presentation* 11:61–68.

———. 1994. "Playing Spaces for Shakespeare: The Maddermarket Theatre, Norwich." *Shakespeare Survey* 47:81–90.

Hodges, C. Walter. 1947. "The Globe Playhouse, Some Notes On a New Reconstruction." *Theatre Notebook* 1 (July): 108–11.

———. 1950. "Unworthy Scaffolds." *Shakespeare Survey* 3:83–94.

Hotson, Leslie. 1954. *The First Night of* Twelfth Night. London: Rupert Hart Davis.

———. 1960. *Shakespeare's Wooden O*. New York: MacMillan.

Kohler, Richard C. 1983. "Vitruvian Proportions in Theatre Design in the Sixteenth and Early Seventeenth Centuries in Italy and England." *Shakespeare Studies* 16:265–325.

Malone, Edward. 1790. "An Historical Account of the English Stage." In *The Plays and Poems of William Shakespeare*, vol. 1, pt. 2, 1–331. London. Reprint 1968, New York: AMS Press.

Nelson, Alan H. 1994. *Early Cambridge Theatres: College, University, and Town Stages, 1464–1720*. Cambridge: Cambridge University Press.

Stinson, James. 1961. "Reconstructions of Elizabethan Public Playhouses." In *Studies in the Elizabethan Theatre*, ed. Charles Prouty, 55–124. Hamden, Conn.: Shoe String.

Styan, J. L. 1959. "The Actor at the Foot of Shakespeare's Platform." *Shakespeare Survey* 12:56–63.

———. 1967. *Shakespeare's Stagecraft*. Cambridge: Cambridge University Press.

# The Mannerist Space in Early

# *Commedia dell'Arte* Iconography

## Paul C. Castagno

THE MANNERIST SPACE of early *commedia dell'arte* iconography will be considered in its sociopetal, informal mode, for wherever the *comici* donned the mask became the site of performance. While this freewheeling statement may seem untenable, in the actual images, spatial relations were conventionalized according to the category, genre, or technical abilities of the artist.

Mannerism is a historical period existing in Europe from 1520 to 1620, centered in Italy with a number of foreign manifestations during which a characteristic style emerged. The Mannerist style is typically exaggerated, distorted, lacks compositional unity, substitutes rhythmical effects for harmony and balance, utilizes figural crowding, elevates *il effetto meraviglioso* (the marvelous effect), promotes spectator orientation, obscures spatial relationships, and possesses other definable traits that distinguish it from the classicistic Renaissance style (Castagno 4). *Maniera* will be considered as an aesthetic concern, particularly in Mannerism's mature development (after 1550), or what Arnold Hauser has called second-generation Mannerism, the period during which the *commedia dell'arte* emerged (44). *Maniera* defines an approach to the making of art that celebrated virtuosic display in execution, albeit based on conventionalized figuration, composition, and topoi. *Bella maniera* indicates the widespread practice of synthesizing multiple sources to achieve the best example of a particular type. For instance, rather than draw directly from the live model, an artist might study Botticelli for faces, Raphael for the grace of pose, another artist for ornament, a fourth for costume, and so on. These elements were then combined into an idealized figural form, which might be used several times in a given painting. The great *bella maniera* artist was able to integrate diverse sources in a strikingly new manner, while still allowing the viewer to reflect on the traces of the original sources.

## The Mannerist Concept of Space

Lack of spatial definition or spatial ambiguity characterizes much Mannerist art. Walter Friedlaender asserts that "unlike the High Renaissance which favored a common harmony of figures and space, in Mannerism the volumes of bodies displace the space, that is, they create the space" (8). This phenomenon contrasts with the Serlian model, which celebrated the stage as a mirror of the city and promoted perspective as a means of describing man's harmonious relationship to a clearly defined and illusionary space. Renaissance stage designers utilized perspective as a visual corollary to "man is the measure of all things" by determining and restricting the proportional field between the three-dimensional figure and the two-dimensional ground. On the other hand, the Mannerists manipulated perspective and proportion to achieve various effects or, as will be seen, to obfuscate spatial depth.

Many early *commedia dell'arte* images demonstrate excessive crowding on the frontal plane, with multiple characters configured into arbitrarily placed groups. This spatial crowding relates to the phenomenon of *horror vacui* in much Mannerist art. Hauser posits that *horror vacui* is associated with the practice of "overfilling the whole picture so that the effect is similar to that of a tapestry with a crowded ornamental pattern" (193). *Horror vacui* also describes vacant areas of negative space that are juxtaposed to areas of crowded figuration—a commonplace in early *commedia* images. An outcome of *horror vacui* is the division of the image into separate nonintegrated parts; that is, each bunched group is isolated as a part rather than harmonized toward a unified whole. Where a strong effect of depth is desired or inevitable, the space is not constructed in the Renaissance sense as a necessity for the bodies but often "is only an incongruous accompaniment for the bunches of figures, which one must read together by jumps in order to reach the depth" (Friedlaender 9). Thus, Mannerist images generally offer multiple points of focus. Compositions often place relatively minor figures in positions of major impact. In the *commedia dell'arte,* this foregrounding reversed expected importance in performance by promoting the minor or divergent over the principal and dramatic—thus the emphasis on the lazzi of the *comici,* or the tour de force of the *innamorata,* over the dramatic plot.

Mannerists characteristically strove for a rhythmical versus static or reposed composition. Rather than seek balance and harmony, the Mannerists juxtaposed figural contours and poses into a network of contrasting, yet visually pulsating shapes. The gestural attitude of the figure shifted from the asymmetrical modulated balance of the Renaissance *contrapposto,* to the Mannerist *figura serpentina,* in which extreme twists in carriage could be noted in a single figure or grouping. The *figura serpentina* subverted the hegemony of the single viewing point, one which had promoted the humanist site of personality: the face. The highly energized spatial field created a new theatrical phenomenology in which gesture, rather than facial expression, became primary. Indeed, for both the Mannerist artists and the *comici dell'arte,* gesture assumed an autonomous, artful purpose that undercut narrative continuity or rhetorical convention, substituting instead exaggerated or distorted body areas—such as hands, limbs, torso, or buttocks, breasts, and phalli—as topoi. For the *commedia dell'arte,* the exaggerations and distortions of the body articulated a newly vibrant theatrical space.

Concomitantly, the changing emphasis from face to body led to the typification of facial features. Obviously, the masks of the *commedia* accomplished something similar, and by directing emphasis below to the limbs the *comici* cleared the way for gestural experimentation while exploiting what Bakhtin has described as the grotesque lower body stratum (148–60).

## The Erotic Space

Eroticizing the space between spectator and performer was a concern of both Mannerists and the *commedia dell'arte;* exploiting this tension underscores one of the major concerns in the arts of the late-cinquecento—that is, an emphasis on, and reification of, the subjective reaction of the spectator, rather than on the art as object. Accordingly, Ferdinando Taviani posits that the eroticized *innamorata* was the major fascination in the early troupes of *commedia dell'arte* and was largely responsible for their great commercial success (42).

## Il Effetto Meraviglioso

Significant to an understanding of space in early *commedia* iconography is the notion of the marvelous effect. In several cases, the *effetto* was achieved through the technique of *trompe l'oeil* (fool the eye), a painterly device whereby two-dimensional figures or objects set in close relief create a lifelike illusion. An effect of immediacy is achieved through the lack of depth behind the figure and the degree of realism that the painter is able to achieve. Representative of this effect are the frescoes at the Rittersaal in Trausnitz Castle, commissioned by Duke Albert V and completed in 1576 by the Flemish painter Federico Sustris. Earlier, Sustris had worked with the great Italian Mannerist Giorgio Vasari in the execution of the frescoes at the Palazzo Vecchio (Hauser 252).

The frescoes of early *commedia* scenes in the stairwell of Trausnitz Castle offer an excellent example of the Mannerist *effetto meraviglioso.* Cesare Molinari succinctly describes the effect: "who[ever] ascends the staircase must have the sensation that the scenes of the *commedia* are unfolding before his eyes" (53). Moreover, the perspective of the person ascending the architectural staircase is disoriented by the view of the two-dimensional painted figures that climb and descend the illusory stairs. Herein, Sustris has created a visual pun. The spectator-oriented design gives the sense of a *commedia* performance in the round, as it seemingly obliterates the boundary between spectator and audience. The painted architectural backgrounds, which often contradict the actual structure upon which they are painted, demonstrate scenic painting techniques in the handling of marble and brick. These effects confirm Würtenberger's claim that the Mannerist frescoes were influenced by scene painting techniques (138–39).

Figural and spatial proportions are ambivalent in many scenes. An example from the Trausnitz fifth wall, south, depicts the monumental figure of the zanni, set in relief against the panel, dwarfing both Pantalone and the mule. The effect of relief is emphasized by the rounded, rhythmical shape of Pantalone's exaggerated humpback, which overlaps the lines of the painted wall. The scene has multiple points of focus: from the lazzo of the bellows of the ass, to Pantalone's reception of the gourd, to the incident at the top of the stairs. Here, the wizened procuress turns away from the action in response to Pantalone's right-handed *noli me tangere,* a gesture of hauteur that warned inferiors away (Castagno 155).

Sustris's compartmentalization of action is enhanced, as niches and doorways are utilized as proscenium frames for the characters. The closed sense of space gives the impression of a series of narrow stages in front of which those who view the frescoes are spectators at a theatrical performance taking place before them.

## *Commedia* Images in the *Maniera* Tradition

Several types of *commedia* images are clearly related to a *maniera* tradition. As earlier indicated, *maniera,* the etymological root of Mannerism, has several applications. *Maniera* seeks to improve upon earlier models or upon nature through *licenzia* (artistic license) or *pratica* (execution), rather than draw its inspiration directly from life. In another sense, it can describe an aspect common to a collective of artists.

Thus, the *maniera* of Fontainebleau suggests a specific approach to painting the figure that brought about the cult of the nude as well as distinctive, virtuosic displays of veiling. *Bella maniera* defines an artistic practice whereby a single image is apparently derived from diverse sources, with the end of achieving the best of its type. For better or worse, the *maniera* artist generally combined the conventional, the anachronistic, and the truly innovative in the process of making art.

As compositional practices increasingly became conventionalized, emphasis was placed more and more on innovation in technique or style. The formalization of methods and techniques is prescribed in works such as Vasari's *Vite* or his *Zibaldone,* or in Karel van Mander's *Schilder-book.* The compositional basis for many Franco-Flemish carnival feasting images is derived from van Mander's dictums. A non-*commedia* print depiction, *The Prodigal Son,* executed in the 1580s by Jacques de Gheyn demonstrates this influence (Davis, Pl. 112). The semicircular arrangement of figures and high vanishing point or horizon line form the basis for similar feasting scenes with *commedia dell'arte* figures. The aspect of simultaneity, the synchronic juxtaposition of sequential data, is distinctive in Northern European Mannerist iconography. The upper left quadrant depicts the final site of the prodigal's ruin—he is sent running from the brothel while being doused with the waste from a chamber pot. In the central, or "present," scene, the main character of the prodigal is barely evident as the focal point yet, on closer inspection, is clearly revealed as the target of Cupid's arrow. The sense of crowding and multiple points of focus are established by the placement of various groups of figures involved in separate, disparate actions. A number of the faces are apparently derived from the same type, while the figural sprawling of the musicians is a commonplace for schemes of this type. In what was the standard for Northern European art of this period, de Gheyn has presented a *vanitas* scene, or moral message, which warns against the dangers of squandering resources and indulging the senses.

Two *commedia* images offer some similarities to the de Gheyn. The painting *Banquet in the Open* (fig. 14) is by Toeput, also called Pozzoserrato, who worked in Tintoretto's workshop in Venice and resided in Treviso (Katritzky 79). Toeput substitutes *commedia* figures for the jesters, establishes the semicircular arrangement around a table, and sets the scene on an Italian hillside with a village in the distance. The spatial and surface qualities of the landscape are *più di maniera, che di natura* (more derived from the artist than nature). Indeed, the entire scene appears to be a stage setting rather than the imitation of an outdoor scene. In the upper left quadrant at a distance, a bull-baiting by a group of *vagabondi* associates the scene with carnival. Pictorially, this group is indexically linked to the zanni in the middle plane, thus utilizing the

Fig. 14 Lodewyk Toeput (Ludovico Pozzoserrato), *Banquet in the Open,* 39.4 × 54.6 centimeters, panel, c. 1590 (Permission of Witt Library, Courtauld Institute of Art, University of London)

commonplace of simultaneity—as in de Gheyn's *The Prodigal Son*—to connect the zanni with the peripatetic nature of the *comici* as vagabonds.

In the most elegantly rendered version of this same image, the Flemish artist Johannes Sadeler tranforms the scene (fig. 15) into an emblem of admonition by adding the caption "*Crapula e Lascivi*" ("Debauchery and Lasciviousness"). Apparently, Sadeler was responding to the demands of the Counter Reformation against scenes of baccanal. Thus, new iconographic codes prevail—for example, the fowl prominently displayed by the food server signifies "your goose is cooked." The church being constructed in the distance contrasts with the secular indoor feasting; the fruitful work of the laborers outside juxtaposes with the decadence and indulgence inside. Inscribed as a teleological image, the theatrical space of the comedians transforms into an antiworld ruled by *il diavolo*. As an emblem of admonition it represents a visual corollary to the *negativa poetica*—the sum of the treatises and tractates written against the *commedia dell'arte* by the fathers of the Counter Reformation (Taviani introduction).

The division of the space into figural groupings defines the space as

Fig. 15 Johannes Sadeler, *Crapula e Lascivia,* 21 × 17 centimeters, engraving, late 1590s (From Douce Portfolio.E.2.6.item 221, permission of Bodleian Library, University of Oxford)

Mannerist, as do the architectural standards, which are enigmatic. For instance, the perspective hallway (upper right) would have to be set farther to the right to work in a practical sense. The effect serves to push the figures toward the frontal plane. Clothing has been updated on the women, but the bare-breasted insouciance in the manner after Clouet has been retained.

Another variation of this scene by Marten de Vos (Katritzky 117) maintains a compositional arrangement almost identical to those of Sadeler and Toeput, altogether eliminating the de Vos's value as a documentary record (Castagno 186). *Maniera* conventions impose a number of caveats on the theatre historian who attempts to define historical moments or personages in the early images.

## Figuration and the Spatial Field

A number of Franco-Flemish images of the comedians place figures on a narrow frontal plane in an almost friezelike manner. Any sense of atmospheric space is voided. The narrowed sense of pictorial space simulates the abbreviated depth of the mountebank stage, where figuration itself created the spatial field.

A painting in the Béziers Museum (probably Francois Bunel, 1585) demonstrates a neat depiction of light and shade that defines the planes broadly while allotting a feeling of monumentality and plasticity. The melodious arabesque of gesture is achieved through the topos of the hands and the overlapping planes. The hand play narrates Pantalone's cuckolding, suggested by the zanni who pulls his beard, thus pointing to the folly of the old suitor by exposing his rotting teeth. The courtesan passes a note to her lover, possibly just given to her by Pantalone; if so, the disclosure of its contents will bring him further ridicule. The placement of Pantalone's left hand is significant. The *maniera* device of indicating while looking elsewhere links the two halves of the composition as it associates Il Magnifico to the bare-breasted courtesan.

The interplay of light and shadow heightens the effect of an intrigue as it enhances the surface quality of the painting. The lighting is Mannerist because it illuminates minor background figures, such as the head in profile and the procuress, while leaving the major figure of Pantalone in relative shadow (Sterling 35).

Elongation, particularly in the proportion of the necks, is reminiscent of treatments by Parmigianino and Primaticcio. The impassive facial expression of the central *innamorata* was a favored style in the 1570s and 1580s at Fontainebleau; it recalls the Fontainebleau painting *Sabina Poppea*, currently housed at the Musée d'Art et d'Histoire, Geneva. If the baring of breasts was relatively common in *commedia dell'arte* performances, it was the *de riguer* fashion at Fontainebleau.

Another famous painting from the Fontainebleau is entitled *Woman Choosing between Two Ages* (fig. 16). In this elegantly rendered painting, an *innamorata*-type is attired only in a transparent veil adorned with pearls (Sterling 25). The transparent veil serves to heighten the erotic effect. The veil was a common topos of *maniera* painting (and poetry). It even came to be seen as equivalent to the notion of allegory. Like the allegory, the veil conceals, although it simultaneously calls attention to what it conceals (Murrin 56–75). This paradoxical union of opposites is representative of the Mannerist *discordia concors*.

The topos of the hands offers a marvelous display of technical execution and a clear indication of narrative. Pantalone makes the sign for his intention to have sexual intercourse, while the *innamorata* hands him his glasses—to see reality as it really is. The pince-nez glasses stress the age differentiation. Meanwhile, the male lover places his right hand unabashedly upon the woman's breast as her right index finger touches her thumb suggesting her intent of compliance. His lips seem about

Fig. 16 Fontainebleau School, *Woman Choosing between Two Ages,* 46 1/8 × 67 inches, c. 1570–75 (Permission of Muséé des Beaux-Arts et d'Archéologie de Rennes)

to contact her neck or whisper an amorous word. The background presents an ambiguous spatial field, the focus of the composition accented by the diagonal joglike flat molding behind Pantalone.

Some common features link these works, as full and profile views intermix. The modeling is more in the manner of *rilievo* than in creating a rounded, dimensional sense. In typical Mannerist fashion, the disposition of figures makes up the space, and any sense of depth is abbreviated. In fact, the lack of depth creates the bizarre illusion that the profiled head in the center of the Bézier springs from the back of the procuress. Now coded as two-faced deceit, the two-headed image was actually a commonplace of early *commedia* iconography—represented in the comings and goings of the wandering comedians by the god of carnival, Janus, whose image is eternalized in the *impresa* of the Gelosi, the most famous troupe of *commedia*'s Golden Age. Furthermore, the two-faced image corresponds to the conflation of the *attrice/meretrice* in the literature of the Counter Reformation. Like the actress, the prostitute played the evanescent roles that pleased her audience.

In both paintings, *sprecher* figures, or those who look out from the painting seemingly at the viewer, appear (Greenwood 55–56). Zanni, the procuress, and the courtesan appear to be soliciting our reaction in the Bézier painting. The *innamorata* in *Woman Choosing* openly solicits our gaze. These *sprecher* effects create an ambivalent subjective relation-

Fig. 17 Franco-Flemish Artist, *The Actors: Scene from the Commedia dell'Arte,* State No. 688, 46 9/16 × 58 1/8 inches, c. 1595–1605 (Permission of the John and Mable Ringling Museum of Art, Sarasota, Florida)

ship between the spectators and the painting, at once focusing our attention while delimiting our level of emotional involvement. Similar to the Jacobean commentator, the *sprecher* charges the spatial field between the spectator and character. Through involvement of the spectator's participation and reaction they serve to metatheatricalize art. Like the actual performances of the *commedia dell'arte,* these paintings seem to acknowledge or integrate spectator response within the spatial field and overall design.

A remarkable painting of a *commedia* scene, *The Actors* (fig. 17) offers a further evolution in this type of scene. Here, the boy with the ringtoss is the *sprecher,* yet through the invention of the artist, the boy directs our eye away from the action (outside the dramatic space). Of course, distraction is a function of the pickpocket's game. The action of the boy *sprecher* posits the contrast between the gypsy who distracts zanni from his purse and the child who distracts us from the theft, while referring us back to our own world outside the painting.

Similar to the Bézier, *The Actors* employs the Mannerist device of crowding the frontal plane and voiding any notion of atmospheric space. Nonetheless, the lack of representational specificity in terms of place is ultimately, and quintessentially theatrical. As a kind of "black box," the space posits the essential theatrical relationship between the actor and the audience. However, there are significant differences from the previous two paintings. The modeling of figures and refined sfumato technique creates a sense of volume that anticipates the baroque. Furthermore, the lighting is consistently directional from the left and seemingly natural, as it accents the edges of the head pieces and the hands of the zanni. Unlike the earlier works in which hands were part of the overall surface treatment, the zanni's left hand projects almost into the spectator's space. This innovation adds a baroquelike sense of dimensionality to the painting.

On the other hand, the refined elegance and preciosity in the execution of the zanni's hands, which contradict his lowly position and background, are demonstrative of contemporary *maniera* techniques. The dichotomy between *pratica* and subject matter, so much a part of the *maniera* tradition, was a problem the baroque artist would attempt to resolve.

## Depth and the Spatial Field

Two distinctive works demonstrate a deeper projection of the spatial field, including a sense of foreground, midground, and background. On a strictly historical level, Leandro Bassano's *Carnival February* (fig. 18) is significant because it is one of the few extant paintings of the early *commedia* by an Italian.[1]

A brief interpretation is as follows: Pantalone, with a fowl strung to his robe, attempts to accost a masked woman (*innamorata*), who is being serenaded while a masked cupid crosses in front. The latter image had a number of connotations related to infidelity and sin. This image is contradicted by the dog figure representing fidelity, although the monkey directly beneath Pantalone indexically establishes the folly of Il Magnifico. To the right of the couple, on a two-step platform, is a zanni figure in a grotesque, serpentine pose, with a kerchief dangling tail-like from his buttocks.

Unique to this Mannerist portrayal is the sense of double vision achieved by Bassano's segmented use of background space. In the rear right quadrant, on a kind of semicircular platform stage, a second Pantalone, the zanni, and tumbler perform a scene in front of a few spec-

---

[1] Unlike Northern European artists, Italian painters considered genre scenes of this type beneath their status as artists. Religious or historical subjects were considered worthy of their attention, and, of course, so was portraiture.

Fig. 18 Leandro Bassano, *Carnival February*, 140.5 × 155 centimeters, late 1580s (Permission of Staatliche Schlösser und Gärten Potsdam-Sansouci, Bildergalerie)

tators. The angular juxtaposition of these two Pantalones denotes what Sypher posited as the "shifting planes of reality" (214–15). On a pictorial level, a strong diagonal tension is created across the surface of the painting heightening the sense of depth.

Is this a shift in performance reality? Is the Pantalone in the foreground performing within a theatrical setting, or is he simply engaged in a genre scene of carnival? The eavesdropper in the upper window of the casa reinforces the sense that this is a theatrical scene, as does the Pantalone-zanni exchange in the upper right quadrant.

The high vanishing point of the perspective gives the design a Serlian sense. Another convention of scene design is the series of steps that separate the foreground from background areas. The bifurcation of space and the flatness of background forms suggest that the frontal actions are played in front of a backdrop, rather than integrated into a representational, three-dimensional scheme.

Yet, the multiple carnival images indicated by the fresh game, available drink, and bull-baiting up center suggest a more liminal modality. Ultimately, the multiple phenomenological levels resonate as a visual pun, punctuating an *effetto meraviglioso* created by the shifting planes of reality. Thus, Bassano succeeds in juxtaposing a grotesque world of mixed narratives and forms within the context of his Mannerist vision.

While Bassano's painting utilized the high vanishing point associated with the tipped perspectives of Serlio, Jacques Callot lowered the horizon line and utilized Mannerist techniques to achieve remarkable depth in his etching. An important characteristic, overlooked by most historians studying Callot's *Balli di Sfessani* series, is the small size of his etchings. Almost exclusively reproduced in a larger format, the actual etchings measure only $2 \frac{3}{4} \times 3 \frac{5}{8}$ inches, or $7 \times 9.2$ centimeters. This limited size emphasizes their preciosity. Preciosity is an attribute of Mannerist art related to exquisite detail and refinement of execution, or suggesting an intricate, elegant structure. Yet, the stunning impact of these etchings derives from the powerful force and monumentality that is captured within these limited perimeters. Callot's virtuosity exalts the contrast between the restricted perimeters of the actual print and his designs, which unfold a vast panorama.

Rather than achieve a sense of space through perspective, Callot overlaps parallel planes in which scale and value are progressively reduced. Callot's figural framing techniques create highly stylized effects. In figure 19, for example, Spessa Monti's legs frame the midground players, while Bagattino's buttocks delineate the action at midground. This framing technique, in which the human form achieves the grandeur of architecture, is indicative of the high level of artifice in Callot's etchings.

Often, the background scenes are more compelling than the major actions on the frontal plane. Callot has no consistent strategy for delineating characters other than to use the varied groupings as stepping stones to delineate space. In a number of plates, Callot arranges the spectators into groupings of three, four, or five figures and places them intermittently about the middle plane. Usually, three or more groups are placed in between the figures on the frontal plane, and a single group or figure is placed on each outer flank. Occasionally, a conventionalized tree, a group of rocks, or a building frame the secondary scene. Their lighter value gradations create a further sense of depth. By extending their arms horizontally to the picture plane and pointing toward the secondary actions, Callot's groupings serve a dual compositional function of focusing the background action while indexically linking us to the major figures on the parallel frontal plane. The low vanishing point and the extreme diminution of figures in the background heighten the effect of panoramic space. Perhaps Mannerism's greatest exemplar of virtuosity, Callot represents the persistence of Mannerism into the seventeenth century.

Fig. 19 Jacques Callot. *Cap. Spessa Monti and Bagattino* from *Balli di Sfessania,* State No. 8092, 2 3/4 × 3 5/8 inches, 1621 (Permission of the John and Mable Ringling Museum of Art, Sarasota, Florida. Gift of A. Everett Austin, Jr.)

Ultimately, it is futile to pinpoint one clearly categorical assessment of Mannerist space in these representations. At its core, the artists were steeped in a *maniera* tradition that promoted conventional approaches in matters of composition and figuration but allowed for a wide range of flexibility in terms of execution and individual technique. Whether on stage or in the studio, this period represents the age of virtuosity; it was the function of the artist or actor not to be the most originally creative but rather to summon their talent, skill, and gusto for the purpose of stimulating the spectators' response.

## Works Cited

Bakhtin, Mikhail. 1968. *Rabelais and His World.* Trans. Helen Islowsky. Cambridge: MIT Press.

Castagno, Paul. 1994. *The Early Commedia dell'Arte (1550–1621): The Mannerist Context.* New York: Peter Lang.

Davis, Bruce. 1988. *Mannerist Prints.* Los Angeles County Museum of Art.

Friedlaender, W. 1957. *Mannerism and Anti-Mannerism in Italian Painting.* New York: Schocken.

Greenwood, John. 1988. *Shifting Perspective and the Stylish Style: Mannerism in Shakespeare and his Jacobean Contemporaries.* Toronto: University of Toronto Press.

Hauser, Arnold. 1965. *Mannerism: The Crisis of the Renaissance and the Origins of Modern Art.* London: Routledge and Kegan Paul.

Katritzky, M. A. 1987. "Lodewyk Toeput and Some Pictures Related to the *Commedia dell'Arte.*" *Renaissance Studies* 1:71–125.

Molinari, Cesare. 1985. *La Commedia dell'Arte: un arte per il teatro.* Milan: Arnoldo Mondadori.

Murrin, Michael. 1969. *The Veil of Allegory.* Chicago: University of Chicago Press.

Ringling Museum Archival Collections, Sarasota, Florida.

Sterling, Charles. 1943. "Early paintings of the commedia dell'arte." *Bulletin of the Metropolitan Museum of Art* 2, no. 1:11–32.

Sypher, Wylie. 1955. "Mannerism." In *Four Stages of Renaissance Style: Transformations in Art and Literature.* New York: Doubleday.

Taviani, Ferdinando. 1969. *La Commedia dell'Arte e la società barocca: La fascinazione del teatro.* Rome: Bulzoni.

Würtenberger, Franzsepp. 1963. *Mannerism: The European Style of the Sixteenth Century.* London: Weidenfeld and Nicolson.

# The Spanish Buen Retiro Theatre,

# 1638–circa 1812

## John Dowling

THE SPANISH *corrales,* in particular the two Madrid public thea-
tres, the Corral de la Cruz and the Corral del Príncipe, have
become familiar to scholars through the efforts of John J. Allen. Al-
though admiration for Allen's scholarship may combine with an ardu-
ous passion for the Spanish theatre to warp our vision romantically, it
is evident that those two playhouses were poor affairs: they were open
to heat, cold, and rain; they had dirty floors; they were crowded and
without seats for a large part of the audience. In short, they were not
places for spectators to wear their best clothes.

Yet, only sixty years after the founding of those two public play-
houses, and at no great distance away, Madrid had constructed a new
court theatre building that was as elegant and technically advanced as
any to be found in Europe. It was built as a part of the *Buen Retiro*
(good retreat)—the new palace in the royal seat of the same name situ-
ated at the eastern edge of Madrid.[1]

In order to grasp the geography of the situation, one may make a
schematic plan by placing a blank sheet of paper in a landscape position
and drawing a vertical line down the middle from top to bottom, la-
beling it N and S. To the west of this line lay the city of Madrid, with
a population in the 1630s of 150,000, twice that of twenty years be-
fore. To the east was mostly open country with only a few structures.
Now, one may draw a horizontal line across the middle of the page and
label it E and W. Imagine that along the western edge and across the
bottom of the page flows the Manzanares River, so paltry a stream that

---

[1]The translations in the text are mine unless there is an already commonly accepted
version.

the satirist Quevedo called it an "apprentice river" (879). However, on the western side of the city, where cliffs rose above the river, was the Alcázar, a fortress palace that housed the king of Spain when he stayed in Madrid. For rest and recreation he could, without disrupting the work of the court, travel east along the route marked by the line. He could go by the *Calle Mayor* (great street), pass on his right the *Plaza Mayor* (great square), and arrive at the *Puerto del Sol* (eastern gate), which is about a quarter of the way along the horizontal line. Once the eastern entrance to the city, the Puerta del Sol was now at the center.

From the Puerta del Sol one may draw another line that runs from this quarter-way point at a thirty degree angle toward the southeast. This is the *Carrera de San Jerónimo* (Saint Jerome's road). Following along this thoroughfare, and at a short distance to the right, the King would leave behind first the Corral de la Cruz and then the Corral del Príncipe. He then could travel downhill toward the center line on the page, which represents a rivulet that flows toward the Manzanares at the bottom of the page. This is the *Paseo del Prado* (meadow boulevard). Across a broad expanse of walkways with an abundance of shade trees is the *San Jeró- nimo* (Saint Jerome church). Since the reign of Philip II, in the last half of the sixteenth century, the church provided modest quarters where the king could stay and relax after hunting in the open country. The royal seat covered the area in the southeast quadrant of the sketch and beyond. The distance between the Alcázar and the church was about two miles.

In the seventeenth century, during the reign of Philip's grandson Philip IV, a wing was added to the royal apartment at the time of the oath of allegiance ceremony in 1632, when the child prince Baltasar Carlos was recognized (fig. 20, no. 2). Another wing was completed in January 1633.

Through his administrative efforts, Philip II had built the bureaucracy and created the procedures that enabled Spain to govern a dominion upon which the sun never set. His son, Philip III, could not endure such self-discipline. He had recourse to the *valido* (favorite), the permanent prime minister. In 1621, his son, Philip IV, inherited the throne at the age of sixteen and followed in his father's footsteps. His *valido* was a man of uncommon political talent: Don Gaspar de Guzmán y Zúñiga (1587–1643), who became the count-duke of Olivares. Playwright Tirso de Molina described him as architect of the new Spain of the high baroque (Brown and Elliott 13). He had been tutor to Prince Philip; then he served the new king for the greater glory of himself, his family, Spain, God, and church. His method was to cater to the inclinations of his onetime pupil, and now master, by playing on the youth's passion for horses, his taste for the theatre, and his predilection for actresses. Olivares provided the palace east of Madrid where the

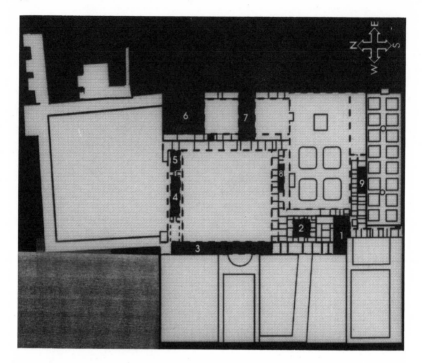

Fig. 20 Plan of the Main Floor of the Palace of the Buen Retiro, based on a plan in Brown and Elliott, *A Palace for a King* (fig. 55, p. 107), which in turn is taken from the 1712 drawings of René Carlier. *Key to numbers:* 1) Church of San Jeronimo; 2) King's Quarters; 3) Landscape Gallery; 4) Hall of Realms; 5) Masking Room; 6) *Coliseo* (Theatre); 7) *Cason* (Ballroom); 8) Queen's Quarters; 9) Prince's Quarters.

young king could take his pleasure—a complex of halls and courtyards worthy of Christendom's greatest monarchy. Thus, a decade after Philip's ascension, Olivares became the architect of a new palace, the Buen Retiro, which would offer young Philip an escape from the gloomy Alcázar on the west.

Construction began in 1633 and moved at a vertiginous pace under the direct supervision of the *valido,* who paid daily visits to the site. The new wings and courtyards were expanded from the earlier additions to the Saint Jerome church. The royal family, and especially Philip, frequently used the new structures for various diversions, such as masques, plays, pageants, dances, bullfights, tournaments, literary soirees, and banquets. Theatrical events were staged in the courtyards or halls and on islands in the lakes. According to Brown and Elliott, "The court of the King of Spain resembled a magnificent theater in which the principal actor was permanently on stage" (31).

Still, five years after construction had begun, there was no theatre building, and Philip was often tempted to venture incognito to one of the public theatres in the city across the Paseo del Prado. Olivares ordered one to be built; the site chosen made it an appendage of the palace at a point east of the central wing that lay between the two great courtyards (fig. 20, no. 6). Construction started in 1638.

Influential in the planning of the Coliseo, as the Buen Retiro theatre would be known, was the Italian stage designer Cosme Lotti, whose arrival in 1626—five years into the reign of Philip IV—marks the beginning of the Italian style in Spanish court theatre. By 1638, Lotti had staged many productions in halls of the old Alcázar and at the Buen Retiro palace.[2] A hydraulic engineer by training and a specialist in fountains, he was noted for his skill with stage machinery. Moreover, his scenographic skills influenced the design of the new Coliseo, particularly its ability to effect sudden scene changes or transformations and its use of perspective and *trompe l'oeil* to attain realistic effects (Shergold 276).

The Coliseo opened on 4 February 1640 with a performance of *Los bandos de Verona*, a version of the Romeo and Juliet story written by Francisco de Rojas Zorrilla (1607–48), a dramatic poet of Calderón's generation. This first production made little use of the resources in the new theatre building, which would be exploited later.

The most notable difference between the Buen Retiro theatre and the old *corrales* was that it had a proscenium arch in the Italian style; thus, the stage did not project into the auditorium as did those at the Príncipe and the Cruz. The plans of the theatre that have come down to us—dated 1655 and 1712—show a slightly irregular wing of the palace that forms a rough rectangle ninety-five feet wide and one hundred and ten feet from the back of the balcony to the back wall of the stage. We do not have exact measurements for the Buen Retiro, but on the basis of standard door, window, and staircase widths, the American scholar Colin Johnson conjectures that the columned and pilastered proscenium opening measured thirty-one feet, while the first backstage area was eighty feet wide, twenty-six feet deep on stage left, and about two feet deeper on the right. Sometime between 1655 and 1712, a double niche was added at the rear (Johnson 157–58). In its completed form, the niche was twenty-five feet deep and graduated from thirty-five feet to twenty-five feet wide. I surmise that these changes were made in the 1650s, since that decade coincides with the sojourn in Spain of another Italian stage designer, Baccio del Bianco, who also was much enamored of perspective.

---

[2]Shergold gives many details of Cosme Lotti's career in Spain (275–89 and passim).

The 1712 drawing done by René Carlier, who was invited to plan a reconstruction of the entire palace, shows a stage with eleven sets of side wings. The first pair is set five feet behind the proscenium wall, and each wing of the pair measures eleven feet wide. Of the eleven sets of wings, the first five could slide off the stage completely. The next three are in the first recess and the last three in the rear niche. They were operated in slots on the stage floor by means of hand winches under the stage (Massar 368).[3] The perspective was closed by a shutter eleven feet wide. If it were flown, the rear of the theatre could be opened, permitting the audience to see the gardens of the Retiro and, in the distance, a lake, though not the Lago Grande.

In a study of the scenes designed by Baccio del Bianco for a 1653 Calderón play, *Andromeda y Perseo*, Phyllis Massar points out that all the proper tackle existed for aerial theatrical machinery (368). After the musical introduction, a nymph on a silver cloud was lowered through the space between the proscenium and the curtain to sing the opening song. By the same route came Painting on the left and Poetry on the right, and their clouds joined that of Music in the center (369).

The audience's space in the Buen Retiro Coliseo bore resemblances to both the *corrales* and to Italianate theatres. Instead of the makeshift *aposentos* in surrounding buildings, as was the case with the jerry-built Cruz and Príncipe, the Buen Retiro Coliseo had formally designed boxes. There were three tiers of four boxes on either side of the stage, and they accommodated both men and women. Directly facing the stage was the *cazuela* (stewpan), for unaccompanied women spectators. Above and slightly behind was the *luneta* (lunette), a semicircular box furnished for the king and his party. Above it and even with the third tier of boxes was another lunette, occupied normally by the Infantada, or palace guardsmen. At the public theatres, *mosqueteros* (groundlings) stood for the whole performance in the patio, separated from a row of spectators seated on stools immediately in front of the stage. The groundlings were held back by a railing that was called a *degolladero* because it reached the height of a man's Adam's apple and in fancy might cut his throat. In the patio of the Coliseo, spectators sat on low stools or chairs moved in for the occasion. The young ladies of the court, the *meninas,* dressed in *guardainfantes* (farthingales) wide enough to conceal a couple of children, reclined on piles of cushions, as was the cus-

---

[3]Colin Johnson may not have taken into account the machinery under the stage when he described the last six sets of wings: "it would appear that these could not be removed without great difficulty and in some cases not at all unless it were done out of sight of the audience" (158).

tom inherited from centuries of coexistence with their Arab conquerors. The practice would suggest that the floors of the Coliseo were cleaner than those of the public theatres.

In his study of the seating capacity of the Coliseo, Colin Johnson concludes that the boxes were eight feet wide except for those at the two corners, which were five feet wide. They were deep, between thirteen and seventeen feet, but from the second row of a box, the line of sight was poor, and those seated there would have been hard-pressed to view even a third of the stage. Most of the audience was seated on benches in the *cazuela* (about 275 women) and in the upper lunette (about 300 guardsmen). Johnson concludes that a capacity audience would number 950 to 1,000 spectators (159–60).

The royal establishment was capable of providing such an audience. Brown and Elliott judge that there were some 400 persons in the central government and 1,700 in the royal household (36). Another 2,000 people were close to the court, among them ecclesiastics, titled nobility, and the foreign community—including the financial contingent. Furthermore, after the king and his courtiers had seen the play, performances were opened to the paying public of Madrid, who resided just across the Paseo del Prado. If the play was produced by one of the companies at the Príncipe or the Cruz, it entered their repertory. If it was a *comedia de tramoya* that required elaborate stage machinery, then that machinery would be moved or reproduced in part, if not in toto, at the public theatres. Thus there developed a symbiosis between the two venues, so that, through Cosme Lotti and later Baccio del Bianco, Italian theory and practice moved into the public theatres and, thereafter, through the movements of actors and managers and traveling companies, to the rest of Spain.

The contract price for the Coliseo was 23,500 ducats at a time when one ducat was considered a good to high daily wage for a laborer (Brown and Elliott 103, 85). If we accept the worth of the ducat at eighty dollars in our time, then the initial cost of the theatre wing of the Buen Retiro palace was $1,880,000. With the overruns typical of construction projects, the cost must have exceeded two million dollars.

The furnishings were luxurious. Visitors wrote of sculptures that adorned the interior of the Coliseo. Prior to the construction of the Coliseo, performances were given in the Hall of Realms, which was adorned with rich hangings as well as with paintings by Velázquez and other contemporary artists (fig. 20, no. 4). One approach to the Coliseo was through the Hall of Realms, which was separated from the theatre by just one room. Because it was sometimes called the "masking" room, it may have continued to be used as an adjunct of the theatre (fig. 20, no. 5).

Scarcely had Romeo and Juliet paced the boards of the new theatre on 4 February 1640 when a destructive fire on 20 February damaged the royal apartments, although it left the Coliseo unharmed (Shergold 300). Nonetheless, the omen was ill for the 1640s. In the summer the Catalans revolted, and in December there was a revolution in Portugal. Cosme Lotti died on 24 December 1643, the queen died the next year, and young Prince Baltasar Carlos died in 1646. During periods of mourning, stage plays were forbidden. Toward the end of the decade, however, court festivities were renewed with the arrival of a new queen, Mariana of Austria. Then, in 1651, at the request of Philip IV, Baccio del Bianco came to Madrid from the court of the grand duke of Tuscany (Massar 365). In modern terms, he was a stage designer and technical director as well as an inventor of theatrical machines. The Coliseo experienced a renewal that lasted until Bianco's death six years later.

During a century and a half more, the Buen Retiro Coliseo experienced periods of glory and years of desuetude. At the beginning of the eighteenth century, Philip V, the new Bourbon monarch, sponsored performances there. He preferred to have a full house when he saw a production and was known to send his guardsmen into the Paseo del Prado and nearby streets to round up spectators to be taken to the theatre, sometimes against their will. The most glorious years were those from 1746 to 1759, the reign of Ferdinand VI and Barbara of Braganza, the melomaniacs (Ponz 6:137).[4] They had continued the employment of Carlo Broschi, Farinelli, the famed castrato who had sung Philip V to sleep every night. Farinelli directed court festivities until he was sent back to Italy by Ferdinand's half brother and successor, Charles III.

The enlightened Charles took governing seriously, but he preferred hunting to any other recreation. However, the Buen Retiro Coliseo did serve enlightened reformers as a channel for their ideas when they created an acting company that specialized in neoclassical tragedy and comedy. The demise of the Coliseo came later during the Napoleonic invasion of Spain.[5] When French troops occupied Madrid in 1812, they

---

[4]Morales Borrero (1972) reproduces illustrations of activities at the Coliseo from a manuscript by Farinelli.

[5]In *El antiguo Madrid,* Mesonero Romanos gives a brief history of the royal seat (2:161–75). As he points out, when fire destroyed the Alcázar in 1734, the court of Philip V was obliged to use the Buen Retiro as their Madrid home. The new palace built on the site of the Alcázar was not occupied until the reign of Charles III, so that Ferdinand and Barbara reigned from the Real Sitio, which they refurbished. Mesonero apparently believed that the *Coliseo* was built during the reign of Ferdinand VI. He also mentions the last years of the Buen Retiro palace in *Memorias de un setentón* (68–109). Although Ferdinand VII repaired the gardens and some structures, most of the palace, including the Coliseo, was too damaged to be easily restored.

were quartered at the Buen Retiro palace, where they wrought destruction that left standing only two buildings of the great complex: the Hall of Realms and the *casón* (ballroom) (fig. 20, nos. 4 and 7). Although it was not the inclination of the sons of the Revolution to spare churches, they also exempted the ancient church of Saint Jerome. Sadly, the Buen Retiro Coliseo did not survive. Today, the area where it once stood is occupied by the typical downtown Madrid building with businesses on the ground floor and apartments above.

## Works Cited

Allen, John J. 1983. *The Reconstruction of a Spanish Golden Age Playhouse: El Corral del Príncipe, 1583–1744.* Gainesville: University Presses of Florida.

Brown, Jonathan, and J. H. Elliott. 1980. *A Palace for a King: The Buen Retiro and the Court of Philip IV.* New Haven, Conn.: Yale University Press.

Deleito y Piñuela, José. 1964. *El rey se divierte.* Madrid: Espasa-Calpe.

Johnson, Colin Bayley. 1974. *A Documentary Survey of Theater in the Madrid Court during the First Half of the Eighteenth Century.* Ph.D. dissertation, University of California, Los Angeles.

Massar, Phyllis Dearborn. 1977. "Scenes for a Calderón Play by Baccio del Bianco." *Master Drawings* 15:365–75.

Mesonero Romanos, Ramón de. 1880. *Memorias de un setentón, natural y vecino de Madrid.* Madrid: La Ilustración Española y Americana.

———. 1881. *El antiguo Madrid. Paseos histórico-anecdóticos por las calles y casas de esta villa.* 2 vols. Madrid: La Ilustración Española y Americana.

Ponz, Antonio. 1782. *Viaje de España en que se da noticia de las cosas más apreciables y dignas de saberse que hay en ella.* Vol. 6 of *Segunda impresión.* Madrid: Joaquín Ibarra.

Quevedo, Francisco de. 1983. "Descubre Manzanares secretos de los que en él se bañian" (1623). In *Poesía original completa,* ed. José Manuel Blecua, 879–82. Barcelona: Planeta.

Shergold, N. D. 1967. *A History of the Spanish Stage from Medieval Times until the End of the Seventeenth Century.* Oxford: Clarendon Press.

# Gothic and Post-Gothic Theatre

## Cities, Paradise, *Corrales*, Globes, and Olimpico

### August W. Staub and Rhona Justice-Malloy

THE ACHIEVEMENT OF a frontal, roofed, and framed theatre, an accomplishment of considerable magnitude, was so radical and ultimately so pervasive, that it led to two assumptions: first, the proscenium frame theatre was unprecedented; second, any prior theatre was unhoused because its practitioners could not think of a way to build a playhouse. Both assumptions need to be reassessed. The framed and roofed theatre, however extraordinary, was part of a long evolution from the ludic and participatory theatre of the Middle Ages; moreover, the medieval theatre deliberately chose *not* to be housed because the very nature of the theatrical concept at that time precluded housing. Many good reasons exist for the need to be unhoused, to be outside.

Medieval theatre was performed on a preempted space, one normally used as a public square or market area, or, in the fairly well-documented case at Romans, in a monastery garden. The preempted space might be a public street corner where pageantry occurred, although pageantry is probably only a variation on the market square theatre. Within the general space (*platea*) are distributed various specific loci of potential action —the several *sedes* or mansions (*sedes* were not always mansions, though mansions were always *sedes*). This generally accepted concept of medieval presentation practice is a direct outgrowth of the cultural assumptions of the era.[1] These cultural assumptions can be described as Gothic because the most dominating icon of the era is the Gothic cathedral.

Aside from the cathedral, Gothic culture as it emerged from the so-

---

[1] Aside from the general histories of theatre, two excellent and thorough studies have been done of the available evidence from medieval theatre: Nagler (1976) and Vince (1984).

called Dark Ages is characterized by the growth of cities, the emergence of a commercial class, and the achievement of a new reliance on the active work of human intelligence over the passivity of an all-encompassing faith. The commitment to human reason was the project of the Scholastic philosopher-teachers associated with the new urban universities. The Gothic cathedral, the city, the establishment of a commercial class, and Scholasticism are all linked; it was commercialism that gave a primacy to human reason, without which neither the building of cathedrals nor the creation of Scholastic philosophy would have been possible. Furthermore, without the development of the cities, there would have been neither the commercial class nor the need for the support and creation of the universities or the erecting of cathedrals.

The realization of the intricate and essential relationship between the city and the several other constituents of Gothic culture is crucial to the understanding of Gothic theatre. The theatre was a major activity of the city, a place where sublime architecture was being constructed and universities were flourishing. Similar to the city from which it grew, Gothic theatre was an event of kinesthetic interchange and participation between player and playgoer, citizen and city, an event organized around tactile, auditory, and motor senses, as well as the sense of sight. Gothic theatre was especially urbane because it partook of the new intellectual life of the city—the university and its Scholastics.

Erwin Panofsky was the first modern scholar to understand the influence of Scholasticism on Gothic arts and, in a brilliant work published over thirty years ago, clarified the tightly woven relationship between the Gothic cathedral and Scholasticism. Panofsky built on the work of Maurice DeWulf, who had made an intriguing case for the interrelationship between Scholasticism and the medieval social and political order. We believe the same relationship prevailed in the theatre. The tenets of the university philosophers are not discussed in the Gothic plays; rather, the relationship is more deeply ingrained as a modus operandi. This inevitable way of doing things derives, or as Thomas Aquinas would say, from "*principium importans ordenem ad actum*" (a shared habit of mind) (1:qu.9,art.3,c.). In order to understand the depth of the relationship, it is necessary to explore the parallels between Scholasticism and theatrical presentation.

These parallels begin with Scholasticism's resolution of the debate between nominalists and realists. The Christian and Islamic neo-Platonic realists had argued that the name of a thing was real because the name encompassed the ideal realization of the thing. The Scholastics, acting in concord with the experience of the commercial class, concluded that names were arbitrary: like prices, reality could vary within the conditions of several items or commodities subsumed under a single name. There was no reality in a word; it was merely the nomination of a class of entities, not the individual thing itself. This concept meant that only things themselves were real. The world did exist and could be approached through its specific Realities, which could in turn be experienced, intellectually sorted, and contemplated. Reason was, therefore, as important as faith. Arriving at such a premise allowed the Scholastics to construct their project of reaching God through the human intellect.

The Scholastic project was organized, like the Islamic theological proposition that had preceded it (DeWulf 283 ff.), to accommodate the problem of the one in the many: the oneness of God through the correspondent accidents of the many individuals. The difference between the new Christian project and its Islamic predecessor was that for the Scholastics, all reality existed in the individual unit, and it was from this unit that one must argue to God. The fundamental approach to this problem was termed *manifestatio,* which means that God is seen clearly through the clarity of his many creations. Thus, the overriding principle is "clarification for clarification's sake" (Panofsky 29–35). Out of this principle, three applied principles developed: (1) understanding the one in the many through totality (sufficient enumeration); (2) relating the one to the many through arrangement (sufficient articulation); and (3) arriving at the one in the many through deductive cogency (sufficient interrelation). These principles provide the foundation for the grand *summae,* the great cathedrals, and the multitudinous theatrical productions of Gothic culture.

Panofsky observed that the architectural tendency in Gothic cathedrals toward transparency is the ultimate spatial realization of *manifestatio.* Similarly, the Gothic theatrical arrangement is an equally compelling spatiokinetic illustration of the habit of clarification. Every spatial possibility, motive, and method for movement is simultaneously present in the production arrangement. Whether we illustrate our theatrical scheme with the ground plan of the Castle of Perseverance, with Fouquet's painting the *Martyrdom of St. Appolonia,* or with later items such as the Cysat layout for the Lucerne cycle or the Valenciennes paintings, there is always the presence of a transparent world. Herein, devils and angels, performers and audience intermingle; the past is simultaneous with present, and free routes of movement are available from one locus to another. The *platea* is at once a place, *the* place, and all possible places. Indeed, the principle of transparency, of clarification, of *manifestatio* may well solve the riddle of the *platea.* The usual explanation that the *platea* was a neutral area might satisfy the modern taste for synchronous logic (i.e., the *platea* was nothing because it was synchronically a larger space for something particular in the locus), but that explanation raises a disquieting question. Why is the *platea* always called the place? The answer is that the *platea* was not neutral; it was truly manifest, at once palpably present and absolutely transparent. More so than the stained-glass windows of a cathedral, the *platea* of the Gothic theatre made space present and lucid. It was the place—seen through all its parts and understood as manifest in all its parts—because it literally contained those parts.

The first subprinciple of clarity is totality, sufficient enumeration of individual realities. This Scholastic principle can be applied to the matter of the *sedes* or loci. Each *sede* is a distinct and private manifestation of the one general concept. Thus, in the *Second Shepherds Play,* the locus of Mak's house is a single, tangible realization of the one concept of marriage, procreation, and birth. The locus of the stable at Bethlehem is yet another tangible presentation of the same concept. The two manifestations are unique and distinct. The one calls up the other, but the one is not the other. Together they enumerate the range of particulars available in the *Second Shepherds Play* for the general concept of nativity. There is one more place of birth—the open field, expressed by the locus of the flock of sheep. These three enumerations make up the many and the one in the earthly world of the performance. Present in the production were probably two figures of the metaphysical world. One would be heavenly and provide the locus of the messenger angel. The other would be infernal and relate to Mak, who may be considered a sorcerer.

Thus, five enumerations are packed into a very brief play. Yet, these five loci complete the total instances available to the Gothic universe. They represent a oneness, but certainly not a unity of place, time, or action. They are a oneness of the total varieties of nativities in a universe composed entirely of angels, devils, shepherds, and the Holy Family. Moreover, it is a multiplicated, particular, and completely sensual oneness, not the formal intellectual unity of the Romanesque or of Islam. In the sensual Gothic world, sheep give birth, shepherds' wives give birth, and Mary gives birth. Heaven marks these events with an angel. Only the devils do not give birth, which is as it should be. This is enumeration sufficient to please any Scholastic. It is, moreover, an enumeration of the life and mentality of the city. For the Gothic city itself contained particular and multiplicated loci, each different from one another yet calling up the others in the oneness of the concept of the encircled city.

The second subprinciple of Scholasticism is arrangement, or sufficient articulation. Again the uses of the several *sedes* offer a theatrical parallel. In Fouquet's *Martyrdom of St. Appolonia* there are at least eight raised loci depicted, with several lower ones implied. Moreover, the painting is clearly a section of a full circle that at least doubles the depicted loci.

The loci are not only treated differently in their architectural headers (some have round canopies, some scalloped, some boxed) but are housing many and very different agents (some are angels, some devils, some musicians, some scholars). In the foreground of the painting is a dazzling variety of distinctly presented figures. There is the saint herself; there is the *maître de jeu;* there are kings and priests and peasants, and even a naughty fellow who has dropped his pants to moon the poor martyr. The mysteries of the wilderness outside the circle of the city are iterated in the presence of wild men and women supporting the berm of the circle. In the background, almost every face and figure is given clear articulation. Theatrical parallels are easily drawn to the highly articulated arguments in a thomist *summa* or to the myriad panes in a cathedral window. This theatrical echo resonates the excitement of the new Gothic experience of urban living, for the city was not the bland unity of rural life but a single place wondrously articulated into many particulars.

Nor is this elaboration of articulations (*partes* and *quaestiones* and *articuli* in the language of the schools) at all chaotic. The whole is held together spatially in the theatrical performance by the *platea,* which provides strong cohesion, and kinetically by the Aristotelian concept of potency-act. According to this concept, each individual locus has the ability to produce inevitable acts that realize the inherent potency of that locus. The locus of the sheep invite, among other things, thievery, otherwise there would be no need for shepherds. The locus of the married household promotes procreation and childbirth, and the locus of Bethlehem has the inherent Christ child.

This kinetic motive of potency-act is also reflected in the pilgrimage, or journey-structure, of Gothic theatre that is implied in the very nature of the *platea* and its several *sedes.* Scenes do not happen in progression in a single space. Rather, both action and actors take journeys, moving with their audience from locus to locus. The scenes do not come to the actors; the actors and their audience go to the scene. This motif of journey is a clear parallel to the third Scholastic principle: deductive cogency, or logical interrelation of parts. Another puzzle presented by Gothic theatre is how any audience can accept an action that commences on a locus only to expand to all parts of the *platea.* How could the Gothic audience understand it otherwise? Does not the acorn progress to the oak? Does not the citizen set out from his or her house to the market and the plaza each day? Does not the pilgrim set out from Stratford to Canterbury, and do not all the miles between finally become the whole, single, and cohesive journey? In short, the logical cogency implied in potency and in the act—so central to the Scholastic explanation of reality as change—finds its counterpart in the production practices of Gothic theatre. If the acorn contains the potential to fill the oak, the citizen to fill the city, and the pilgrim to fill the journey, then surely the *sede* has the potency to fill the *platea*.

Just as the Gothic theatre was of a mind with the Scholastics, the Scholastics were of a mind with the city; for like the cities of which they are a product, the great *summae* teem with varieties of instances, thus adding to a single, contained, and rounded whole. The Gothic theatre and the Gothic city were identical. Both were places of participation, realized not through what was seen but what was said and done. Both were constructed of sufficient loci manifestly joined by an enmuraled *platea*. Both were articulations of God's kingdom.

The image of heaven as a City of God goes back to Augustine, but the concept had lost its application under the feudal system. With the reemergence of cities, first in Islamic societies and then in Christendom, the image of the City of God again becomes viable. Moreover, this is a walled and enchanted city, one that can contain the entire holy place, literally a paradise. Indeed, here the Christian and Islamic visions entwine. The word *paradise* is borrowed from Arabic and literally means "watered garden." In the desert, such a garden could easily be identified with heaven. Islamic mind went some steps further, for its paradises were always miniature cities. They were uniformly walled and carefully laid out in terms of loci and passageways that invite movement as well as rest. The central feature was the water that flowed through a fountain or a pool. Its gardens were living testimony to the Aristotelian concept of potency-act, which was a central tenant of Islamic neo-Platonism, as was the problem of reconciling the One in the many (DeWulf 194–207). As Ardalan and Bakhtiar posit, "The architectural conception of the garden reflects the 'sense of place' . . . encompassing within itself a total reflection of the universe" (68). Alexander continues this same idea: "The action and the space are indivisible. The action is supported by this kind of space. The space supports this kind of action" (69–70). Above any other consideration, the Islamic garden was not an oasis in a desert but a walled paradise in a city, where it reflected in distillation the city that was its raison d'être, and where it became, within its earthly city, the more precious City of God, not God as eternal rest but God as prime mover, first potency of all the earth and the waters.

This is the City of God that the Moors brought to Spain, where they constructed some of the most exquisite courtyard paradises in the world. These courtyards would proliferate into the many *corrales* of the Iberian Christian cities. Some of these *corrales* became theatres, but this was because each *corral* reflected the city in miniature, and because each *corral* was a place of participation where action and space were one, as action and space had been one in the great Gothic theatres.

Indeed, the *corrales* theatres of Spain, the innyard theatres of England (later made into specific playhouses) and such structures as the Teatro Olimpico in Vicenza may all be called post-Gothic theatres, for they are all participatory spaces based on the mentality of the Gothic city with its many loci, its cohesive plaza or *platea*, and its walls of magic encirclement. "This wooden O," says Shakespeare; "this Globe."

How much richer this pun is than ever could be imagined! The Globe was unroofed because it was first and foremost a garden, a walled city, a ludic and participatory place. Imagine the Fouquet painting superimposed on the deWitt sketch of the Swan Theatre, for surely deWitt left out all the spectators who were distributed about the walled circle of the theatre—sitting on the playing area (the *platea*) as was no doubt their custom in any Gothic or post-Gothic theatre. The two spectators that climb a pole in Fouquet's painting exhibit the participatory nature of the attendees, their inclination to become part of the act and potency. This inclination constitutes the whole argument of the *Knight of the Burning Pestle,* and convinces Hamlet that he can entrap the king. This participatory nature of an entirely ludic and kinetic theatre has too long been neglected. For example, in Elizabethan theatre, debate over the use of scenery has predominated any consideration of the participatory audience. Yet, the active audience was the primary scenery, while the city was the audience's reason for existing. The potency of the city provided the potency of the theatre. Illusion was not a factor in the playhouses and *corrales* of the post-Gothic theatre.

The real achievement of the Teatro Olimpico was not as the first permanent proscenium structure of the Renaissance; rather, it was primarily another paradise, a brilliant example of a walled garden. Palladio downplayed those aspects of the Olimpico that today seem most prized. Certainly, it was a roofed structure, but the domed ceiling recalls the dome of the heavens (and was later painted to resemble the sky). Teatro Olimpico does in fact contain framed perspectives, but these are cityscapes, not interiors. Moreover, they present several loci of an ideal urbanity, a city of God, encircled by the *teatro* itself. To complete the image of a walled city, the circle of the audience is complemented by a final circle of statuary mounted as sentinels on the city walls. These statues represent the citizens of the production. The *platea* is an open thoroughfare—a place potent with action and participation. The Teatro Olimpico is ultimately a post-Gothic "O," a globe containing the "One in the many."

Lope de Vega's theatre was a walled garden, Shakespeare's Globe was a walled city. Palladio, with Scamozzi, also built an enmuraled city. All three theatres were under the sky and thus reflected the condition of the city. They invited audience participation because that is the nature of a city. Furthermore, the plays written for such theatres employed the *sede-platea* structure because that is also the condition of the city. Later in the seventeenth century, when the many of the city are replaced in importance by the one of the court, a visual, roofed theatre will take ascendancy. However, this change will be slow and uneven. Louis XIV was still participating in *comedie-ballet* long after the city had been replaced by the *salle* and the one-roofed, protected, and idealized body of the king had been substituted for the many, varied, and particularized bodies of the city. When a single part of the king's body—the royal eye—was given privilege, the Gothic period withered, and a room was substituted for paradise, but not before England and Spain had created golden ages of drama that gestated in the hurly-burly of post-Gothic theatre.

## Works Cited

Alexander, Christopher. 1979. *The Timeless Way of Building*. New York: Oxford University Press.

Ardalan, Nader and Lalek Bakhtiar. 1973. *The Sense of Unity: The Sufi Tradition in Persian Architecture*. Chicago: University of Chicago Press.

DeWulf, Maurice. 1922. *Philosophy and Civilization in the Middle Ages*. Princeton: Princeton University Press.

Nagler, A. N. 1976. *The Medieval Religious Stage*. New Haven: Yale University Press.

Panofsky, Erwin. 1957. *Gothic Architecture and Scholasticism*. Cleveland: World Publishing Company.

Thomas Aquinas, Saint. 1994. *Summa Theologica*. Trans. William P. Gaumgarth. Scranton, Penn.: University of Scranton Press.

Vince, Ronald W. 1984. *Ancient and Medieval Theatre*. Westport, Conn.: Greenwood Press.

# Academic Theatricality and the Transmission of Form in the Italian Renaissance

## Thomas F. Connolly

A N EXAMINATION OF the intellectual and academic basis of the Italian Renaissance drama, exclusive of the *commedia dell'arte*, demonstrates why it was never a popular form. It was unpopular because it emerged from a heuristic, almost hermetic tradition that was inaccessible to the illiterate majority of the Italian people and of limited interest to the literate minority. Thus, any analysis of the persons responsible for the *commedia erudità* is dealing with a minority of a minority. Nevertheless, it is possible to make broad assertions about the legacy of the learned drama that demonstrate how its humanist ideology provided the basis for the bourgeois drama of the late baroque.

The *commedia erudità* and its predecessor, the Latin humanistic comedy, are often cited as part of a tradition that dates from the classical era (Radcliffe-Umstead 59–63). The motivations responsible for the self-conscious development of humanistic and erudite plays may be seen as indicative of the sort of intellectual strivings that brought together the scholarly associations called academies. Some academies were more like collegial clubs than formal schools, while others were organized quite regularly with faculties and student bodies (Oosting 102). Regardless of organizational formality, the academy members were especially interested in rhetorical exchange, through which ideas were transmitted, received, or commented on. The Renaissance academicians institutionalized Italian intellectual and rhetorical development, culminating an ideological and linguistic debate that had its roots in the High Middle Ages. In 1331, Petrarch had experimented with dramatic imitations of Terence in order to perfect the means by which his ideas could be transmitted. However, he was not satisfied with these results and later destroyed them. Petrarch lamented that it was impossible to create dramatic works that were equal to the plays of the ancients.

Petrarch's dramaturgical inadequacy was echoed by another would-be dramatist, Leon Battista Alberti. Alberti shared Petrarch's concerns about the proper function of language. Alberti's quattrocento dialogues developed the rhetorical debate as an academic form that paralleled the refinement of the Italian language. In 1433, a century after Petrarch's experiments, Alberti composed Italian imitations of the Ciceronian dialogues. Also in 1433, Donatus's commentary on Terence was rediscovered; as a result, many scholars were inspired to create Latin dialogues. Yet, by publishing his dialogues in Italian, Alberti elevated the Italian language as appropriate for scholarly discourse. Alberti felt he was doing for the Italians what Cicero had done for the ancient Romans: making foreign knowledge accessible. Whereas Cicero adapted Greek models, Alberti adapted Roman sources (Marsh 79).

Before these attempts, Alberti had written the play *Philodoxus* (c. 1426) in Latin. Both his dialogues and the play have the same moral concerns—that is, what constitutes civic duty, and what the role of marriage in society is. Alberti was concerned with how his moralizing would be received. While the dialogues are allowed to speak for themselves, the play has an appended commentary that explicates the characteristics of the play's Latin idioms, revealing it to be an essentially moral comedy. The play concludes with a double wedding, a standard convention of later erudite comedies and pastoral dramas. Alberti annotated his play because he presented it as an actual Roman comedy by "Lepidus." His ruse was successful for ten years, until he revealed the truth about the play's authorship. The play by "Lepidus" had been taken quite seriously; nevertheless, the play by Alberti was dismissed as a flawed, hopelessly inadequate, modern imitation (Radcliffe-Umstead 31). Thus, by 1436, one intellectual of the Italian Renaissance had innovated an idea toward a new sort of drama, but remained uncertain as to the means. Because literary theory lagged behind dramatic practice, it was some time before an adequate explanation of dramatic form emerged. Would-be playwrights did not have a forum to test their works, for the academies were not yet willing to sponsor theatrical productions.

However, there was an event in 1443 that spurred the development of Italian drama. A manuscript containing fourteen comedies by Plautus, twelve previously lost, became available to Italian readers. This manuscript, the *Codex Ursinianus,* was discovered in Germany by an Italian cleric in 1428; it soon was coveted by notable figures such as the Pope and the king of Naples. Although it took fifteen years for copies of the text to be disseminated (Radcliffe-Umstead 60), the discovery of the Plautine texts doubled the number of Roman comedies (six by Terence and six by Plautus had been extant). This event was "electrifying to the world of humanism" (Radcliffe-Umstead 59). Burckhardt posits that such an increase in *exempla* for academics and men of letters may have led to the "first impulse for the public representations of these plays" (1:258). Whatever the specific impulse may have been, during the following decades the Roman plays became models for new Italian plays. In 1520, Paolo Giovio lamented that Plautus and Terence have been "banished to make room for Italian comedies" (Burckhardt 1:246).

Giovio's lamentation was grounded in the old belief that plays are only useful as rhetorical tools. However, by the turn of the century, the authors of humanistic comedies were more interested in ideas than in rhetorical exchange as an end in itself. The possibility that the Italian language was as useful as Latin represented the realization of a new idea. The half century or so between the first performance at the Teatro Olimpico and the composition of *Il Pastor Fido* represents a historical incubation of an intellectual aesthetic. The Teatro Olimpico performance of *Il Pastor Fido* demonstrates the reification (via the theatre) of what intellectuals sought: a language of their own to equal that of Plautus and Terence.

From a late-twentieth-century vantage point, it is easy to assess the traditional niche occupied by the Italian Renaissance academies in theatrical historiography; they are worth considering because a noted academy happened to sponsor the construction of the Teatro Olimpico. The extant structure itself inspires inquiry, rather than why it was built or why a group of academics was serious about drama. Its architecture not its ideology is all that matters. Similarly, *Il Pastor Fido* is regarded as a phenomenon that precipitated a literary quarrel rather than as an intellectual response to the development of the pastoral drama. Thus, an examination of the first academic production of Terence's *Andria* at the Accademia Olimpica illustrates the academy's need to theatricalize dramatic ideas, as Guarini's tragicomic *Il Pastor Fido* represents an attempt at realizing a perfectly dramatic ideal.

The Accademia Olimpica in Vicenza, first chartered in 1555, was part of an academic tradition that had existed since the end of the fourteenth century. The Olimpica of Vicenza was one of the more structured academies, ostensibly a finishing school for gentlemen striving to become the *uomo universale*. Yet it was not so much the universal man that these academies were molding but men of the universe—men who sought to place themselves beyond the civil or ecclesiastical constraints, men who found Scholasticism too polite and classical models simply inadequate for the range of their scientific, artistic, and literary endeavors. For example, the use of Italian by academic playwrights is significant not only because it was frowned on by schoolmen and clerics but also because the linguistic perfectionism of an academic such as Trissino, whose *Sofonisba* of 1515 was written in such polished Italian that most people would have been unable to understand it, brought to drama in the Italian idiom what Petrarch and Alberti had attempted earlier in Latin.

Academic drama showcased a learned argot by an elite that saw itself as above all other groups, not merely separate but distinct. Its distinction can be noted from its creation of two new forms: the pastoral and the tragicomedy. Moreover, Vicenza's several academies provide a glimpse of the "privileged" versus the "free and secret" academies that coexisted at this time. This clarification underscores the developing separation between academicians of high scientific ideals and dilettantes.

Before the Olimpica was chartered, there were two academies in Vicenza: the Academy of the Sociniani (1536) and Trissino's Accademia di Vicenza (1538). The Socinianian academy was founded by Lelio Socino, a student of ancient languages and literatures. Socino, who secretly espoused Lutheranism, was abetted by a disciple, Fulvio Pellegrino Morato, who was not content to blaspheme *in camera* and became quite notorious for his stridently anti-Papist views. As a result, relations between Rome and Vicenza became so strained that Pope Paul III cancelled the council that had been scheduled for Vicenza in 1538.

Giorgio Trissino's institute was founded in 1538, while the Sociniani were embroiled with the Vatican. During this year, Trissino completed Villa Cricoli with the assistance of Andrea Palladio. The scholarly rigors imposed by the anachronistic classicism of Trissino leads to problematic conclusions, as an examination of the routine at Trissino's institute bears out:

> Study, Arts and Virtue—these key-words—embraced the program of the Academy. Students lived at Cricoli (Trissino's villa) and their work was regulated from day break to nightfall. Trissino seems to have wished to blend the ideals of monastic life with the traditions of the Greek schools of philosophers. Strict moral codes as well as physical cleanliness were peremptory demands. The study of Latin and Greek, guiding the student to an accomplished Italian style, was the medium through which he hoped to infuse . . . virtues into the young generation. (Wittkower 60)

The goal of this rigorous academic training was an accomplished Italian style that would refute Trissino's "anachronistic and dogmatic classicism." Indeed, Trissino was against "any popular tendencies toward adaptive classicism" (Wittkower 69). Trissino's *La Poetica* of 1529, in addition to its translations and commentary on specific passages in Aristotle, is a philological polemic for an idealized Italian language opposed to the *volgare*. Unlike the hot-blooded heretics of the Socinianian academy, the thoroughly orthodox Trissino sponsored pedagogues such as Trebazio, whose translations of Aristotle's *Politics* and *Ethics* were praised as models of erudition by Pope Paul III during the Council of Trent.

Whatever their differences regarding the Pope or the regulation of members' daily routines, the academies were primarily learning centers with programmed curricula. The Accademia Olimpica was made up of twenty-one fellows who "were varied in their professions [or specializations] [and] were singular in their purpose" (Oosting 103). Each member wanted to learn about science and, especially, mathematics. For the academicians, a *matematico* was not merely a student of numbers but one who interpreted numbers as an alphabet of first causes: the key to cosmology and theology. The preamble of the academy's statutes describes mathematics as "the true ornament of all those who had the noble spirit and virtue" (Oosting 103).

The activities of the Accademia Olimpica were eclectic. Within months of its inauguration on 30 March 1556, the founding Belli family gave a series of lectures on mathematics; on 8 June 1556 Silvio Belli gave a lecture on Plato. On 23 December 1556 plans were undertaken for "the recitation of a comedy under the name of the Academy to which each member could bring three guests" (Oosting 104). A month later, the plans were codified by the academy's governance into a new statute that described the function of dramatic performances as primarily for the education of the academicians. The statute further promulgated the means by which a *commedia* was to be produced. Four academicians were elected to make provisions for and arrange the scenery; five were in charge of the costuming; and another academician was in charge of the music. The academy's members were to be proportionally responsible for the expenses. The head of the academy recommended the "*sala di San Marcello* as the place where the *scena* should be put in order" (Oosting 104), although the court of the academician, Elio Belli, was ultimately used.

On 23 February, with the statutes now in place, four academicians were charged with securing the area of the *scena* (stage) and the *apparato* (scenery and machinery) (Oosting 104). Three days later, Girolamo da Schio was appointed as director of the theatrical performance, and the mayor of Vicenza was notified that "all possible and necessary provisions had been taken in order that the comedy might be performed peacefully" (Oosting 104). The notice is significant since it describes the performance as taking place in a private home, under the auspices of a chartered organization. The *Andria* was performed, using Alessandro Mazzaria's Italian translation, sometime between 26 February and 8 March 1557. Civic officials were assured of peace during the comedy's performance, which took place over carnival week (Mitchell 187). From the academy's records, little information can be ascertained about the production except that it was received with "great satisfaction and pleasure of all the audience" (Oosting 105). Lumber had been purchased for construction in preparation for the performance and the academy voted to pay for it on 28 February 1558—a year after the performance. Since Elio Belli's palazzo is no longer extant, and no plans remain, the nature of the playing space remains indeterminate. Thus, the actual decor by the painter, Giovanni Fasolo, and the sculptor, Lorenzo Rubini, is a matter of speculation.

The details of the Olimpica's first theatrical reveal an intellectual approach to drama representative of Accademia Olimpica's approach. The intent of theatrical performance was neither to entertain nor to sanctify, although the production seems to have inadvertently given pleasure.

Emphasis on legitimization of form is crucial to the Renaissance. While the elitist hegemony of the academies and courtiers was by no means monolithic, it is still possible to determine how and when a dramatic form was legitimized. The academies had standards that they felt were necessary to preserve the classical forms. On the other hand, the rigidity of these new standards transmitted form rather than preserved it. Thus, the transmission of classical values from the eclogue (a poem in dialogue or soliloquy form) to the pastoral represents the creation of a new dramatic genre out of a literary one. In terms of dramatic form, a more humanistic approach can be seen in the development of the tragicomic pastoral.

Pastoral drama, rather than tragedy or comedy, loomed the largest in the academies of the Italian Renaissance. The influence of Vergil and the Latin poets was the primary reason, although it was not simply that the Italians had no Greek influence and therefore got caught up in Latin classicism. While they had Senecan tragedy to imitate, Trissino actually wrote his *Sofonisba* to promote the Greek type of tragedy, and it was, after all, Sophocles' *Oedipus Rex* that was translated for the Teatro Olimpico, not Seneca's. However, the eclogue derives from Vergil's bucolics. Dante, Petrarch, and Boccacio revived the form in Italy, where it parallels the development of the Italian language.

What was in the pastoral that made it such an appropriate mode for the academic dramatists of the Renaissance? Pastoral drama is concerned with the conscious juxtaposition of the natural with the artificial, the perfection of the nearly perfect. It is also secular, despite the presence of divine or semidivine figures, as these nonmortals are merely dramatic figurations of divinity rather than representatives of a higher spiritual order. This notion that pastoral is the perfection of the nearly perfect culminates in Guarini's *Il Pastor Fido*. Tragicomic pastoral is the ideal Renaissance genre because it represents the triumph of humanism as applied to drama. Guarini defends himself in his *Verrati* against all charges of impropriety by citing the scientific control that he, as author, is able to exercise over the audience of his drama (Weinberg 2:1087–88). Thus, the personal emotions of Guarini's characters are something that will exert a control over the audience and ensure a reasoned and reasonable catharsis of which the audience will be conscious. Guarini's control as a humanist over his text is extended via that text to include his audience's reasonable catharsis. The importance of individual feeling that Guarini stresses in *Il Pastor Fido* is especially significant because the paramount emotion of, and motivating factor for, the play's characters is romantic love.

The concerns of the play are love and justice. The lovers are triumphant, and the evildoers are punished. Silvio and Dorinda, and Mirtillo and Amarilli are united. Mere circumstance is the cause; mistaken identity and misplaced children are accidents that can be remedied. Neither fate nor divine vengeance is employed or alluded to: human effort and a humane consciousness pervade. Guarini is the chief defender of this new genre, asserting that

> it acknowledges its first origin in the eclogue and in the ancient satyr play whence its characters came, in its form and order [though] it can be called a modern poem. . . . He who composes tragicomedy takes from tragedy its great personages but not its action, its verisimilar plot but not one based on truth, its emotions aroused but their edges abated, its delight but not its sadness, its danger but not its death; from comedy laughter that is not riotous, modest merriment, feigned complication, happy reversal, and above all the comic order. (Herrick 138)

Order is thus seen as the primary aim of this genre; tragicomedy's resolution is the return to order. Nevertheless, tragicomedy was not immediately embraced by the professional scholars who routinely arbitrated such matters, and a controversy sprang up over *Il Pastor Fido* before it was ever performed or published. In 1587, an archetypal schoolman, Giasone Denores, professor of moral philosophy at the University of Padua (the center of Italian Aristotelianism), attacked Guarini's work for being a disunited aberration. Undoubtedly, Denores felt that Guarini was a traitor to his class, since thirty years earlier the playwright had been professor of rhetoric at Padua. (Guarini had also served as secretary to the Eterei Academy in 1564.)

Guarini responded to Denores's attack a year later with the first *Verrato*. This rebuttal began a famous quarrel that would last for years and not be resolved until Denores's death in 1590, the year the play was published. It is not the literary aspect of pastoral tragicomedy that is significant here; rather, it is the lingering acrimony between the university-trained scholars and the independent academies. That such a dispute could arise as late as the 1580s involving a professor and an upstart playwright—a man guilty of not acknowledging his learning or morality—suggests that Scholasticism died a much slower death than is generally supposed. One thrust of Denores's attack was that the lives of shepherds were of too little consequence to interest an urban audience. This demonstrates how little he understood what the play actually concerned.

The High Middle Ages and early Renaissance adequately rediscovered classicism but, as seen in the cases of Petrarch and Alberti, did not adequately develop drama into modern forms. Guarini felt he successfully realized this development with his pastoral tragicomedy. The modernity of the Olimpica's production lies with its formulaic and intellectual approach to the drama. The production of the *Andria* had no official civic or religious function, nor was it specifically to entertain; it was a manifestation in form and content of certain intellectual impulses felt by the academicians. I do not mean modern in a positivistic sense; rather, it indicates the meaning of modernity in a Renaissance context. Perhaps the most important transmission from the Olimpica to Guarini is the attitude that with an adequately ancient grounding, something contemporary may be transmitted beyond the merely neoclassical. The modernizing element is the means by which dramatic form is transmitted in the Renaissance through the play of ideas. Thus, drama becomes a vehicle, its form encompassing and transmitting an intellectual tradition.

## Works Cited

Burckhardt, Jacob. 1929. *The Civilization of the Renaissance in Italy.* 2 Vols. Illustrated edition. New York: Harper and Row.

Conradi, Edward. 1905. "Learned Societies and Academies in Early Times." *Pedagogical Seminary* 2:12–43.

Corrigan, Beatrice. 1972. "Italian Renaissance Drama and its Critics: A Survey of Recent Studies." *Renaissance Drama,* new series, 5:191–211.

Doran, Madeleine. 1954. *Endeavors of Art: A Study of Form in Elizabethan Drama.* Madison: University of Wisconsin.

Herrick, Marvin. 1962. *Tragicomedy.* Urbana: University of Illinois.

Marsh, David. 1980. *The Quattrocento Dialogue: Classical Tradition and Humanist Innovation.* Cambridge: Harvard University Press.

Martines, Lauro. 1979. *Power and Imagination: City-States in Renaissance Italy.* New York: Alfred A. Knopf.

Mitchell, Bonner. 1971. "Circumstance and Setting in the Earliest Productions of Italian Comedy." *Renaissance Drama,* new series, 4:185–97.

Oosting, J. Thomas. 1981. *Andrea Palladio's Teatro Olimpico.* Ann Arbor, Mich.: UMI Research Press.

Radcliffe-Umstead, Douglas. 1969. *The Birth of Modern Comedy in Renaissance Italy.* Chicago: University of Chicago.

Schrade, Leo. 1960. *La représentation d'edipo tirano au Teatro Olimpico.* Paris: Editions du Centre National de la Recherche Scientifique.

Weinberg, Bernard. 1963. *A History of Literary Criticism in the Italian Renaissance.* 2 vols. Chicago: University of Chicago.

Wittkower, Rudolf. 1965. *Architectural Principles in the Age of Humanism.* New York: Random House.

# Contributors

*Luigi Allegri* chairs the Department of Theatre and Film History at the University of Parma, Italy. His books range from a history of medieval theatre (*Teatro e spettacolo nel medioevo*) to a study of society and theatrical space (*Teatro, Spazio, Società*).

*John J. Allen* is Professor of Spanish and Italian at the University of Kentucky. He is president of the Cervantes Society of America and author of *Don Quixote: Hero or Fool?* His other books include *The Reconstruction of a Spanish Golden-Age Playhouse* and a co-authored book on the Spanish playhouses, *Los teatros comerciales del siglo XVII y la escenificacion de la comedia.*

*Paul C. Castagno* directs the New Playwrights' Program and heads the M.F.A. Playwriting/Dramaturgy Program at The University of Alabama. He published the book, *The Early Commedia dell'Arte (1550–1621): The Mannerist Context,* and has authored articles for *NTQ, Theatre Topics, Journal of Dramatic Theory and Criticism, Theatre History Studies,* and others.

*Thomas F. Connolly* teaches at Suffolk University. He is currently book review editor for *Theatre Research International* and has published articles in the *Cambridge Guide to American Theatre* and the *Blackwell Companion to 20th-Century Theatre.*

*John Dowling* is Alumni Distinguished Professor Emeritus of Romance Languages and Dean Emeritus of the Graduate School at the University of Georgia. He is the author of many works dealing with the Spanish theatre from the Golden Age through the twentieth century.

*Andrew Gurr* is a New Zealander who has worked mainly in Britain for the last thirty years. He has published the very influential *Shakespearean Stage, 1574–1642*, along with a number of other books through Cambridge University Press. *The Shakespearean Playing Companies* is forthcoming from Oxford University Press.

*Franklin J. Hildy* (conference co-director) is on the faculty of the Department of Drama at the University of Georgia. His books include *Shakespeare at the Maddermarket: Nugent Monck and the Norwich Players* (1986) and *New Issues in the Reconstruction of Shakespeare's Theatre* (1990). He served on the Advisory Council of the Shakespeare Globe Trust and is deeply involved with the reconstruction of the New Globe.

*Rhona Justice-Malloy* serves on the faculty of the Department of Drama at the University of Georgia. Her publications include the article "Charcot and the Theatricalization of Hysteria" in the winter 1994 issue of *Popular Culture*.

*Stanley V. Longman* (conference co-director) teaches playwriting, theatre history, and dramatic criticism at the University of Georgia. He authored *Composing Drama for Stage and Screen* (Allyn and Bacon) and several articles and chapters in books on dramatic theory and criticism. He has published a number of articles on Italian theatre history. Professor Longman will be the next editor of *Theatre Symposium*.

*Frank Mohler* is on the design faculty of the Department of Theatre at Appalachian State University. He has a strong interest in historic theatre and has done extensive research on the scenery and machines of the Italianate theatres.

*Thomas A. Pallen* is on the theatre faculty at Austin Peay University. His book *The Theatre Historian's Guide to Vasari* has been accepted for publication by Southern Illinois Press.

*Virginia Scott* is a Professor of Theatre at the University of Massachusetts. She is the author of *The Commedia dell'Arte in Paris*, which won the 1991 George Freedley Award. She recently completed her tenure as a Camargo Fellow in France, where she wrote the first half of a new biography on Molière.

*August W. Staub* has served for many years as the Head of the Department of Drama at the University of Georgia. His books include *Introduction to Theatrical Arts* (1972), *Creating Theatre: The Art of The-*

*atrical Directing* (1973), and *Varieties of Theatrical Art* (1980). He is the past president of the American Theatre Association and National Association of Schools of Theatre.

***Ronald Vince*** teaches theatre history and literature at the McMaster University. He has published three definitive works on the historiography of European theatre before 1800. He is currently writing a book on performance in the ancient world.